HOW DO I MAKE...?

A Hands-On Guide to Cooking Anything (& Everything) You Love

W9-BYL-305

TASTE OF HOME BOOKS • RDA ENTHUSIAST BRANDS, LLC • MILWAUKEE, WI

Taste of Home

© 2018 RDA Enthusiast Brands, LLC.
1610 N. 2nd St., Suite 102, Milwaukee WI 53212.
All rights reserved. Taste of Home is a registered
trademark of RDA Enthusiast Brands, LLC.

EDITORIAL

Chief Content Officer: Beth Tomkiw
Creative Director: Howard Greenberg
Associate Creative Director: Edwin Robles Jr.
Vice President, Content Operations: Kerri Balliet

Managing Editor, Print & Digital Books:
Mark Hagen
Associate Editor: Molly Jasinski
Art Director: Raeann Thompson
Graphic Designer: Courtney Lovetere
Layout Designer: Sophie Beck
Copy Chief: Deb Warlaumont Mulvey
Copy Editors: Dulcie Shoener (senior),
Ronald Kovach, Chris McLaughlin, Ellie Piper
Contributing Copy Editors: Michael Juley,
Valerie Phillips
Editorial Services Manager: Kelly Madison-Liebe
Editorial Production Coordinator: Jill Banks
Editorial Intern: Stephanie Harte

Content Director: Julie Blume Benedict
Food Editors: Rashanda Cobbins; James Schend;
Peggy Woodward, RDN

Culinary Director: Sarah Thompson
Kitchen Operations Manager:
Bethany Van Jacobson
Recipe Editors: Sue Ryon (lead), Irene Yeh
Food Stylists: Kathryn Conrad (senior),
Lauren Knoelke, Shannon Roum
Culinary Assistants: Aria C. Thornton,
Lynne Belcher
Food Buyer: Maria Petrella

Photography Director: Stephanie Marchese
Photographers: Dan Roberts, Jim Wieland
Photographer/Set Stylist: Grace Natoli Sheldon
Set Stylists: Melissa Franco (lead), Stacey Genaw,
Dee Dee Schaefer

Business Architect, Publishing Technologies:
Amanda Harmatys
Business Analysts, Publishing Technologies:
Dena Ahlers, Kate Unger
**Junior Business Analyst, Publishing
Technologies:** Shannon Stroud

Editorial Business Manager: Kristy Martin
Editorial Business Associate: Andrea Meiers
Rights & Permissions Assistant: Jill Godsey

BUSINESS

Publisher: Donna Lindskog
**Experiential Programming & Partnerships
Director, Taste of Home LIVE:**
Jamie Piette Andrzejewski
**Events & Operations Brand Manager,
Taste of Home LIVE:** Jaclyn Miller

TRUSTED MEDIA BRANDS, INC.

President & Chief Executive Officer:
Bonnie Kintzer
Chief Financial Officer: Dean Durbin
Chief Marketing Officer: C. Alec Casey
Chief Revenue Officer: Richard Sutton
Chief Digital Officer: Vince Errico
**Senior Vice President, Global HR
& Communications:**
Phyllis E. Gebhardt, SPHR; SHRM-SCP
General Counsel: Mark Sirota
Vice President, Product Marketing:
Brian Kennedy
Vice President, Consumer Acquisition:
Heather Plant
Vice President, Operations: Michael Garzone
Vice President, Consumer Marketing Planning:
Jim Woods
Vice President, Digital Product & Technology:
Nick Contardo
**Vice President, Digital Content & Audience
Development:** Kari Hodes
Vice President, Financial Planning & Analysis:
William Houston

For other Taste of Home books and products,
visit us at **tasteofhome.com.**

International Standard Book Number:
978-1-61765-723-8
Library of Congress Control Number:
2017952580

Cover Photographer: Dan Roberts
Set Stylist: Dee Dee Schaefer
Food Stylist: Lauren Knoelke

Pictured on front cover:
Best Spaghetti & Meatballs, page 151
Pictured on back cover:
Chocolate Cake with Chocolate Frosting, page
170; Brown Sugar, page 13; Barbecued Picnic
Chicken, page 247; Nanny's Parmesan Mashed
Potatoes, page 302; Midwest Mary, page 16; Slow
Cooker Spinach & Artichoke Dip, page 258

Printed in China.
1 3 5 7 9 10 8 6 4 2

YES, YOU CAN MAKE IT!

If you've ever wanted to make French toast, grilled burgers, chicken noodle soup, holiday ham or chocolate cake but felt too intimidated, let this cookbook be your guide. With *Taste of Home* **How Do I Make...,** we'll walk you, step by step, through all the recipes you've always wanted to master.

Inside you'll learn how to:

- Cook a healthy meal for yourself.
- Wow family and friends with special dinners.
- Bake mouthwatering desserts.
- Use the slow cooker to your advantage.

- Become a grilling pro.
- Host your own happy hour.
- Serve eye-opening breakfasts.
- Create dishes with only five ingredients.
- Determine if meat is properly cooked.
- Poach an egg.
- And much more!

Whether you're a kitchen newbie or you simply need a refresher, the *Taste of Home* Test Kitchen experts created **How Do I Make...** to be your indispensable guide to tackling any kitchen task with ease.

TABLE OF CONTENTS

GET SOCIAL
WITH US!
#TASTEOFHOME

To find a recipe: tasteofhome.com
To submit a recipe: tasteofhome.com/submit
To find out about other *Taste of Home* **products:**
shoptasteofhome.com

LIKE US facebook.com/tasteofhome

TWEET US twitter.com/tasteofhome

FOLLOW US @tasteofhome

PIN US pinterest.com/taste_of_home

THE BASICS

Find out which kitchen tools you should have on hand, how to best measure ingredients and how to stock the freezer, refrigerator and pantry so you can make a meal anytime. Wondering what type of cookware and knives to buy? Check out the handy lists inside. In a pinch and don't have the pan size a recipe calls for? Turn to our bakeware substitution chart for a quick fix!

CHOOSING BAKEWARE

Aluminum pans with dull finishes give the best overall results. Pans with dark finishes often cook and brown foods more quickly. If using pans with dark finishes, you may need to adjust the baking time and cover the tops with foil during baking to prevent overbrowning. Insulated pans and pans with shiny finishes generally take longer to bake and brown foods.

Baking dishes are made of ovenproof glass or ceramic. If you substitute a glass baking dish in a recipe that calls for a metal pan, reduce the oven temperature by 25 degrees to avoid overbaking.

To determine your bakeware's measurements, use a ruler to measure from one inside top edge to the opposite inside top edge. To measure height, place a ruler on the outside of the dish and measure from the bottom to the top edge. To determine volume, fill the pan or dish to the rim with measured water.

For best results, use the pan size called for in the recipe. However, if you don't have the pan specified by the recipe, the chart to the right offers practical substitutions.

PICK THE PERFECT PAN

IF YOU DON'T HAVE THIS PAN:	USE THIS PAN INSTEAD:
One 9x5-in. loaf pan	Three 5¾x3x2-in. loaf pans
One 8x4-in. loaf pan	Two 5¾x3x2-in. loaf pans
One 9-in. round baking pan	One 8-in. square baking dish
Two 9-in. round baking pans	One 13x9-in. baking pan
One 10-in. fluted tube pan	One 10-in. tube pan or two 9x5-in. loaf pans
One 13x9-in. baking pan	Two 9-in. round baking pans or two 8-in. square baking dishes

CHOOSING COOKWARE

Good-quality cookware conducts heat quickly and cooks food evenly. The type of metal and thickness of the pan impact its performance. Here are some pros and cons to each of the most common cookware metals:

ALUMINUM is a good conductor of heat and is relatively inexpensive. However, it reacts with acidic and alkaline ingredients, so it can alter the flavor of such foods.

CAST IRON conducts heat very well, and it fortifies food with iron. These pans need regular seasoning to prevent sticking and rusting.

* See page 77 to learn how to clean cast iron.

COPPER is an excellent heat conductor. However, it is expensive, it tarnishes—requiring periodic polishing—and it reacts with acidic ingredients, which is why copper pan interiors are typically lined with tin or stainless steel.

ANODIZED ALUMINUM has the same good qualities as aluminum, but the surface is electrochemically treated so it will not react to acidic ingredients. The surface is nonstick and resistant to scratches.

STAINLESS STEEL is durable and retains its new look for years. It isn't a great conductor of heat, which is why it often has an aluminum or copper core or bottom.

OTHER THINGS TO CONSIDER Thicker-gauge cookware heats and cooks more evenly than thinner-gauge cookware of the same material. Nonstick surfaces make for easy cleanup and are great for skillets and saute pans, but are not necessary for saucepans and Dutch ovens.

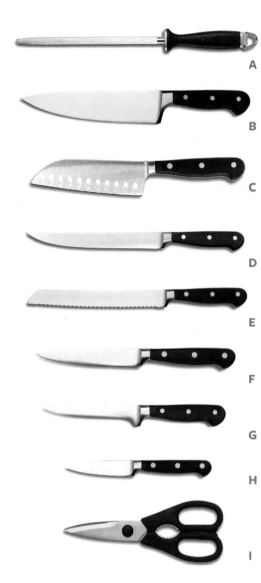

CHOOSING CUTLERY

A basic set of knives is essential to any well-equipped kitchen. There are a variety of styles and materials to choose from. Knives made from high-carbon steel are easier to sharpen and stay sharper longer than those made from stainless steel. They are, however, more prone to corrosion than stainless steel.

A. STEEL Also called a sharpener, this long, thin rod with a handle is used to smooth out rough spots on the edge of a knife blade and to reset the blade's edge.

B. CHEF'S KNIFE This 8- to 10-in. multipurpose knife can be used for such tasks as mincing, chopping and dicing.

C. SANTOKU This is a Japanese variation of a chef's knife. The 6½- to 7-in. multipurpose knife is used for mincing, chopping, dicing and slicing. The blade's dimple design helps reduce drag during slicing.

D. CARVING KNIFE This 8- to 10-in. knife is perfect for slicing roasts and turkey.

E. SERRATED OR BREAD KNIFE This knife's jagged blade is used for slicing breads, cakes and delicate foods. An 8-in. knife is the most versatile, but a range of lengths is available.

F. UTILITY KNIFE This 6-in. knife is a good size for everyday slicing, dicing and mincing.

G. BONING KNIFE This knife's 5- or 6-in. tapered blade is designed to remove meat from poultry, beef, pork or fish bones.

H. PARING KNIFE This 3- to 4-in. knife is used for peeling, slicing and trimming small foods.

I. KITCHEN SHEARS This versatile tool can be used for a multitude of tasks, including cutting twine, snipping herbs, disjointing chicken and trimming pastry dough.

HOW DO I...

CARE FOR KNIVES

- To keep knives sharp, cut foods on a soft plastic or wooden cutting board. Ceramic, granite, metal and other hard surfaces will dull the knife's blade.

- Always hand-wash knives immediately after use. Never let them soak in water or wash them in the dishwasher.

- Store knives in a slotted wooden block or hang them on a magnetic rack designed for knives. Proper storage will protect knife edges, keep blades sharper longer and guard against injury. Do not store loose in a drawer.

HOW TO USE A STEEL

Rest the tip of the steel on the work surface. Hold your knife at a 20-degree angle to the steel. Start with the heel of the blade against the steel and draw the blade up across the steel until you reach the tip of the knife. Repeat five times on both sides of knife blade, alternating sides. Repeat as needed.

GET COOKING WITH A WELL-STOCKED KITCHEN

With a well-stocked pantry, refrigerator and freezer, you'll be able to serve a satisfying meal even when time is tight. Consider having these items on hand:

- A quick-cooking meat or two, like boneless chicken breasts, chicken thighs, pork tenderloin, pork chops, ground meats, Italian sausage, sirloin and flank steaks, fish fillets and shrimp
- Frozen vegetables
- Pastas, rice, rice mixes and couscous
- Dairy products like milk, sour cream, cheeses (shredded, cubed or crumbled), eggs, yogurt and butter or margarine

- Condiments such as ketchup, mustard, mayonnaise, salad dressing, salsa, taco sauce, soy sauce, stir-fry sauce and lemon juice
- Fresh fruits and vegetables
- Dried herbs, spices, vinegars, oils and various seasoning mixes
- Pasta sauces, olives, beans, broths, canned tomatoes, canned vegetables and canned or dried soups

ESSENTIAL KITCHEN TOOLS EVERYONE SHOULD HAVE

STOCK UP!

☐ **Chef's knife:** Treat yourself! Go to a specialty store to find the best match for you.

☐ **Metal and silicone spatulas:** Use a sturdy metal spatula for flipping, tossing and serving up all kinds of foods. Use silicone for scraping out a food processor or down the sides of a mixing bowl, spreading frosting onto a cake or folding whipped egg whites into cake or pancake batter.

☐ **Whisk:** Choose a mid-size whisk with a handle that fits comfortably in your hand.

☐ **Slotted spoon:** A perforated (slotted) spoon acts like a mini strainer, so you can remove foods from liquid but retain the liquid.

☐ **Tongs**

☐ **Kitchen shears:** Use shears to open packaging, snip away herb stems or trim fat from meats.

☐ **Cast-iron pan:** They go right in the oven, so use 'em for making corn breads and cobblers.

☐ **Nonstick skillet:** Easy to clean, lightweight nonstick pans are ideal for frying eggs or wilting greens. Get one with a ceramic coating.

☐ **Saucepans:** Look for a 5- or 6-quart size. A smaller saucepan (1.5 or 2.5 quarts) comes in handy for smaller items, like boiled eggs, rice and oatmeal.

☐ **Dutch oven:** Look for a 5- or 6-quart pan if you cook for a small crew, or go big with 7 or 8 quarts to feed a crowd. This pan can be used in the oven or on the stove.

☐ **Sheet pan:** Sheet pans are fab for baking cookies or one-pan dinners.

☐ **13x9 baking pan:** Bake up a hearty casserole or sweet sheet cake with this versatile dish.

☐ **Colander:** Wash fruit and drain pasta, blanched veggies and other boiled foods. Look for ceramic or metal; both are sturdier than plastic.

☐ **Box grater**

☐ **Microplane:** A fine grater that's perfect for zesting citrus or sprinkling Parmesan over a dish of pasta.

☐ **Prep and mixing bowls**

☐ **Immersion blender:** This hand-held tool allows you to blend soups, smoothies and pestos with the push of a button.

☐ **Instant-read thermometer:** Easily check to see if your meats have cooked enough.

☐ **Chopping block:** A wooden chopping block helps protect your knife from dulling quickly and makes cleanup a breeze.

MEASURING CORRECTLY: THE SECRET TO SUCCESS!

LIQUIDS

Place a liquid measuring cup on a level surface. For a traditional liquid measuring cup, view the amount at eye level to be sure of an accurate measure. Do not lift the cup to check the level. Some newer liquid measuring cups are designed to be accurately read from above.

For sticky liquids such as molasses, corn syrup or honey, spray the measuring cup with nonstick cooking spray before adding the liquid. This will make it easier to pour out the liquid and clean.

SHORTENING

Press shortening into a dry measuring cup with a spatula to make sure it is solidly packed, without air pockets. With a metal spatula or the flat side of a knife, level contents with the rim. Some shortenings come in sticks and can be measured like butter.

SOUR CREAM AND YOGURT

Spoon sour cream or yogurt into a dry measuring cup, then level the top by sweeping a metal spatula or flat side of a knife across the top of the cup.

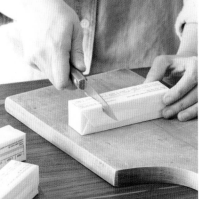

DRY INGREDIENTS

For dry ingredients such as flour, sugar or cornmeal, spoon ingredients into a dry measuring cup over a canister or waxed paper. Fill cup to overflowing, then level by sweeping a metal spatula or flat side of a knife across the top.

SPOON MEASUREMENTS

Pour liquids like vanilla extract into a measuring spoon over a bowl or custard cup. Never measure over the batter, because some may spill and you may end up with too much.

BUTTER

The wrappers for sticks of butter come with markings for tablespoons, ¼ cup, ⅓ cup and ½ cup. Use a knife to cut off the desired amount.

BROWN SUGAR

When a recipe calls for brown sugar, it should always be firmly packed when measuring. The moisture in brown sugar tends to trap air between the crystals; packing the sugar helps remove that air.

✳

TEST KITCHEN TIP

When measuring bulky dry ingredients, such as cranberries, raisins, chocolate chips or oats, spoon or pour them into a measuring cup, then level the top with your hand or a spatula.

HOW DO I MAKE...

COCKTAILS & BEVERAGES

Save money and bring happy hour home! Become your own bartender and learn how to make your favorite drinks. Not in the mood for alcohol? Cool down with an ice-cold glass of homemade lemonade, or start your day off with a simple smoothie or iced coffee drink.

MIDWEST MARY

In the Midwest, Bloody Marys garnished with meats, cheeses and veggies are works of art. My beverage has skewers of brats, cheese curds and dill pickles.
—Kathryn Conrad, Milwaukee, WI

Start to Finish: 15 min. **Makes:** 6 servings

3 lemon wedges
3 tablespoons kosher salt
2 teaspoons coarsely ground pepper
    Ice cubes
3 cups chilled tomato juice
2 cups chilled beer
¾ cup chilled vodka
⅓ cup lemon juice
4 teaspoons hot pepper sauce
2 teaspoons Worcestershire sauce
    Sliced cooked bratwurst links, cheese curds and small dill pickles

1. Using lemon wedges, moisten the rims of six highball glasses. Sprinkle salt and pepper on a plate; dip rims in mixture. Fill glasses with ice; set aside.

2. In a large pitcher, combine tomato juice, beer, vodka, lemon juice, hot pepper sauce and Worcestershire sauce; pour into prepared glasses. Garnish with skewers of bratwurst, cheese and pickles.

✳

TEST KITCHEN TIP
Highball glasses, sometimes also known as Collins glasses, are versatile and are great for serving many cocktails, sodas or beer. You can easily find them online or in most stores where glasses are sold.

ALL-AMERICAN BLOODY MARY

Our version of this classic beverage blends your favorite regionally inspired garnishes. Let the good times roll!

Cheeseburger slider

Wisconsin: If there's one thing Wisconsinites love more than cheese, it's cheese topping a two-bite bacon butter burger.

Deviled egg

North Carolina: In true Tar Heel style, this diabolical delight is made with Mt. Olive brand sweet pickle relish.

Beef stick

Texas: It's what's for dinner—or brunch. Savor this smoky treat from the Longhorn State.

Old Bay seasoning

Maryland: Replace so-so celery salt on the rim with zesty Old Bay.

Soft pretzel

New York: This tender twist is very big in the Big Apple.

Dungeness crab claw

Washington: Take your drink from delicious to delectable by snapping up the sweetest meat in the Pacific Northwest.

CHEERS!

SPARKLING PUNCH

As a table brightener, fix a bowl of festive fruity punch—it's a refreshing beverage you can mix together in moments.
—Karen Ann Bland, Gove City, KS

Prep: 10 min. + chilling **Makes:** 24 servings (3 quarts)

3 cups water

1 can (6 ounces) frozen orange juice concentrate, thawed

¾ cup thawed lemonade concentrate

2 cups cranberry juice cocktail

½ cup sugar

1½ liters lemon-lime soda, chilled

In a large bowl, combine the first five ingredients; mix until sugar is dissolved. Chill for 1-2 hours. Just before serving, stir in soda.

✳

TEST KITCHEN TIP
Chill all punch ingredients before mixing so that you don't have to dilute the punch with ice to get it cold.

WHY YOU'LL LOVE IT...

"I made this for my sister's wedding and everyone LOVED it! It's really fast and easy to make, as well as super delicious. I will definitely make this again."

—GRETLE, TASTEOFHOME.COM

GINGER-KALE SMOOTHIES

Since I started drinking these spiced-up smoothies for breakfast every day, I honestly feel better!
Substitute any fruit and juice you like to make this recipe your own blend.
—Linda Green, Kilauea, HI

Start to Finish: 15 min. **Makes:** 2 servings

1¼ cups orange juice
1 teaspoon lemon juice
2 cups torn fresh kale
1 medium apple, peeled and coarsely chopped
1 tablespoon minced fresh gingerroot
4 ice cubes
⅛ teaspoon ground cinnamon
⅛ teaspoon ground turmeric or ¼-inch piece fresh turmeric, peeled and finely chopped
Dash cayenne pepper

Place all ingredients in a blender; cover and process until blended. Serve immediately.

SMOOTH OPERATORS

Make yours tropical, berry-packed or peachy and creamy. *Taste of Home* Facebook friends share their secrets for adding wholesome ingredients to their sweet smoothies.

Fresh Peach: My smoothies use vanilla almond milk, orange juice, peaches, Greek yogurt and a surprise ingredient: English cucumber.
—Angela L., Conroe, TX

Green Goodness: I make smoothies with frozen or fresh fruit, kefir, spinach and unsweetened almond milk, plus flax and chia seeds. Yummy!
—Jami K., Baltic, SD

Peach Melba: I use frozen peaches, raspberries, yogurt, peach nectar, wheat germ and vanilla to make mine taste like this old-school dessert.
—Mari L., Kalamazoo, MI

Strawberry-Banana: I make a smoothie almost every day for my granddaughter using 1 banana, ½ cup strawberry yogurt, a splash of coconut water and a handful of frozen strawberries.
—Don M., Durand, MI

Sweet Potato-Cherry: There's nothing like a blend of sweet potatoes, banana and cherries.
—Brenda N., Memphis, TN

Coconut-Mango: I combine coconut milk, mango, pineapple, Greek yogurt and ice.
—Megan W., Birmingham, AL

Peanutty Chocolate: With baby spinach, banana, dark chocolate soy milk, dairy-free yogurt, powdered peanut butter, instant coffee granules and ice, this tasty combo is gluten- and dairy-free.
—Tricia W., Oshkosh, WI

Broccoli-Berry: My favorite smoothie includes frozen broccoli, frozen berries, a banana, kiwi, Greek yogurt, fruit juice of some kind and hemp protein powder.
—Lisa M., Peterborough, ON

Mango-Carrot: You can't go wrong with frozen mango chunks, almonds, cinnamon, raw carrot, milk and water. Blend all until smooth.
—Ian C., Deux-Montagnes, QC

Pumpkin Spice: This tastes just like fall: pumpkin puree, vanilla Greek yogurt, orange juice, cinnamon, nutmeg and ice.
—Syndee M., Round Lake, IL

HOW TO MAKE LEMONADE

(Pictured left, top to bottom)

- To get the most juice from the lemons, roll them with the palm of your hand firmly over the counter. Feeling lazy? You can also heat in the microwave on high for 10-20 seconds.

- In a large saucepan, combine sugar, 1 cup water and lemon peel. Cutting back on sugar? Add less if you want!

- Cook and stir over medium heat until sugar is dissolved, about 4 minutes.

- Remove your simmering saucepan from the heat. Stir in the fresh lemon juice and remaining water. Then, pop it into the fridge until it's cold.

OLD-FASHIONED LEMONADE

This sweet-tart lemonade is a traditional part of my Memorial Day and Fourth of July menus. Folks can't get enough of the classic fresh-squeezed flavor.
—Tammi Simpson, Greensburg, KY

Prep: 10 min. **Cook:** 5 min. + chilling **Makes:** 7 servings

1⅓ cups sugar
5 cups water, divided
1 tablespoon grated lemon peel
1¾ cups lemon juice (about 10 large lemons)

In a large saucepan, combine sugar, 1 cup water and lemon peel. Cook and stir over medium heat until sugar is dissolved, about 4 minutes. Remove from heat. Stir in lemon juice and remaining water; refrigerate until cold. Serve over ice.

✳

TEST KITCHEN TIP
To make limeade, substitute lime peel for lemon peel and limes for lemons.

To make lavender lemonade, add 2 tablespoons dried lavender to the sugar and lemon peel mixture before simmering. If desired, strain before serving.

To make ginger-mint lemonade, add 1-2 tablespoons grated fresh gingerroot and 1-2 mint sprigs to the sugar and lemon peel mixture before simmering. If desired, strain before serving.

BLACK-EYED SUSAN

The Kentucky Derby has the mint julep; the Preakness has the Black-Eyed Susan. The drink is a sunny mix of vodka, rum, and pineapple and orange juices to toast your special events.
—*Taste of Home* Test Kitchen

Start to Finish: 5 min. **Makes:** 1 serving

½ to ¾ cup crushed ice
1 ounce vodka
1 ounce light rum
½ ounce Triple Sec
2 ounces unsweetened pineapple juice
2 ounces orange juice
  Lime slice and pitted sweet dark cherry

Place desired amount of ice in a rocks glass. Pour vodka, rum, Triple Sec and juices into glass. Stir; serve with a lime slice and cherry.

HOW TO BUILD THE ESSENTIAL SUMMER BAR

Whether your idea of a great summer day is sipping a cocktail as you watch the fireflies or laughing it up with friends over brunch, here's what you'll need to make sure the bar's ready. Don't worry if you're missing a few items—basics go a long way.

The basics

Classic summer spirits:
Rum • Bourbon or whiskey • Gin • Vodka • Tequila

Build on the base

Keeping a few secondary options around will help you customize your cocktails. Bitters and flavored liqueurs are usually used in small quantities, so a single bottle will log a lot of miles.

Bitters—classic Angostura • Orange liqueur—Cointreau or Grand Marnier • Elderflower liqueur—St-Germain • Ginger liqueur—Domaine de Canton

From the farmers market

Fresh produce, especially celery and tomato • Citrus • Seasonal stone fruits and berries • Herbs

Mixers

Mixers are the nonalcoholic liquid ingredients added to cocktails.

Club soda • Tonic water • Colas and ginger ale • Juice • Simple syrups

The tool kit

An initial investment in a few key items will pay you back for years to come.

Cocktail shaker and strainer • Muddler (or the handle of a wooden spoon) • Ice cube trays • Paring knife • Bottle/wine opener • Peeler • Hand-held citrus press • Straws

BUT FIRST, COFFEE!

EASY SPICED MORNING MOCHA

This recipe is a delicious morning pick-me-up, and it still tastes great when made with low-fat milk.
—Vickie Wright, Omaha, NE

Start to Finish: 10 min. **Makes:** 1 serving

1 tablespoon French vanilla
    powdered nondairy creamer
1½ teaspoons sugar
1 teaspoon instant coffee granules
1 teaspoon baking cocoa
¼ teaspoon ground ginger
¼ teaspoon ground cinnamon
1 cup hot 2% milk or water
    Sweetened whipped cream and
      additional ground cinnamon

Place the first six ingredients in a mug. Stir in hot milk until blended. Top with whipped cream; sprinkle with additional cinnamon.

HOW TO MAKE WHIPPED CREAM

You'll need:
1 cup heavy whipping cream
3 tablespoons confectioners' sugar (you can also use granulated sugar, honey or maple syrup)
½ teaspoon vanilla extract
Chilled mixing bowl
Chilled beaters or whisk

- In a chilled small glass bowl, beat whipping cream until it begins to thicken. It should begin to have some body or "oomph" to it.

- Once the cream is slightly thickened, add the confectioners' sugar and vanilla. Continue beating until soft peaks form (soft peaks are when the whipped cream points curl down when beaters are lifted). The recipe will double in size and become a mound of smooth, sweet whipped cream.

SANGRIA BLANCO

Using white instead of red wine makes my version of sangria a bit lighter, yet with the same wonderful sweetness. Frozen fruit allows me to serve this refreshing sipper any time of year.
—Sharon Tipton, Casselberry, FL

Start to Finish: 15 min. **Makes:** 6 servings

¼ cup sugar
¼ cup brandy
1 cup sliced peeled fresh or frozen peaches, thawed
1 cup sliced fresh or frozen strawberries, thawed
1 medium lemon, sliced
1 medium lime, sliced
1 bottle (750 milliliters) dry white wine, chilled
1 can (12 ounces) lemon-lime soda, chilled
Ice cubes

In a pitcher, mix sugar and brandy until sugar is dissolved. Add remaining ingredients; stir gently to combine. Serve over ice.

SIPPING PRETTY

Add these colorful ice cubes to drinks to make them extra special. Just fill an ice tray with water and pop in fresh herbs, citrus or berries, then let it all freeze.

- **Berries**
  Strawberries • Blueberries • Raspberries

- **Herbs**
  Basil • Mint

- **Citrus**
  Lemon • Lime • Orange

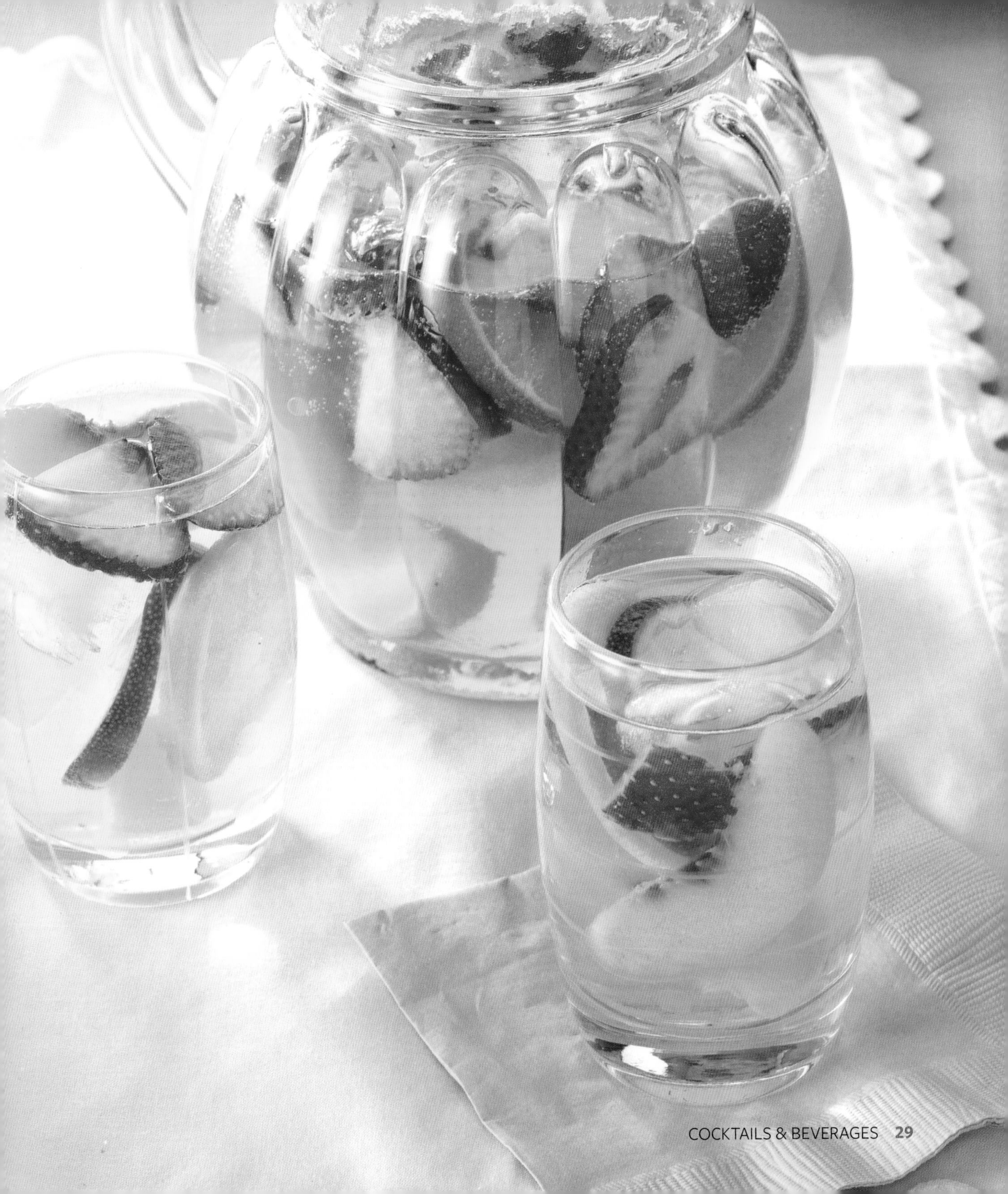

BRANDY OLD-FASHIONED SWEET

Here in Wisconsin, we make this old-fashioned favorite using brandy in place of whiskey and soda instead of water for a milder sweet cocktail.
—*Taste of Home* Test Kitchen

Start to Finish: 10 min. **Makes:** 1 serving

1 orange slice
1 maraschino cherry
1½ ounces maraschino cherry juice
1 teaspoon bitters
¼ to ⅓ cup ice cubes
1½ ounces brandy
2 teaspoons water
1 teaspoon orange juice
3 ounces lemon-lime soda
Maraschino cherry and lemon slice, optional

In a rocks glass, muddle orange slice, cherry, cherry juice and bitters. Add ice. Pour in the brandy, water, orange juice and soda. Garnish as desired.

HOW TO MUDDLE A DRINK

Place aromatic ingredients like citrus or herbs in the glass. Add a small amount of sugar or bitters. With a muddler, gently crush and bruise the ingredients until their aromas are released. An ice cream scoop is a good stand-in if you don't have a muddler.

TEST KITCHEN TIP
Sometimes called an old-fashioned glass, rocks glasses are for, you guessed it, drinks on the rocks. They're also used for drinks that require building the drink inside the glass you're serving it in.

HOW DO I MAKE...

APPETIZERS & SMALL PLATES

Let's get the party started! Mix and match these snacking-approved recipes and you'll be the best host ever! Invite friends over to watch a game, binge-watch the latest show or just chat and eat together.

DILL VEGETABLE DIP

A friend gave me this zesty dip recipe many years ago, and now I serve it at our annual holiday open house. To make it mobile, spoon a serving of the dip in the bottom of a disposable cup, then garnish with fresh veggies.
—Karen Gardiner, Eutaw, AL

Prep: 5 min. + chilling **Makes:** 1½ cups

1 cup (8 ounces) sour cream
½ cup mayonnaise
1 tablespoon finely chopped onion
2 teaspoons dried parsley flakes
1 teaspoon dill weed
1 teaspoon seasoned salt
Assorted fresh vegetables

Combine the first six ingredients; mix well. Cover and refrigerate. Serve with vegetables.

HOW TO PREP A PEPPER

(Pictured right, top to bottom)

- Cut top and bottom off pepper and throw those parts away. Cut each side from pepper by slicing close to center and then down. Scrape out seeds and discard.

- Cut away any ribs (the thick white part inside the pepper that holds the seeds).

- Place skin side down and flatten slightly with your hand. Cut lengthwise into strips or as recipe directs.

WHY YOU'LL LOVE IT...

"My family now prefers this to the traditional buttermilk dressing dip. The only thing I changed was to replace the finely chopped onion with 1 teaspoon of dried minced onion. Great recipe."

—SPROWL, TASTEOFHOME.COM

HOMEMADE
DIP!

SAUCY ASIAN MEATBALLS

This meatball recipe originally called for beef and pork and a different combination of seasonings.
I used ground turkey and altered the seasonings to create a healthy, fresh-flavored variation.
—Lisa Varner, El Paso, TX

Prep: 20 min. **Bake:** 20 min. **Makes:** about 3 dozen

1 pound lean ground turkey
2 garlic cloves, minced
1 teaspoon plus ¼ cup reduced-sodium soy sauce, divided
½ teaspoon ground ginger
¼ cup rice vinegar
¼ cup tomato paste
2 tablespoons molasses
1 teaspoon hot pepper sauce

1. Preheat oven to 350°. Place the turkey in a large bowl. Sprinkle with garlic, 1 teaspoon soy sauce and ginger; mix lightly but thoroughly. Shape into 1-in. balls; place in a 15x10x1-in. baking pan. Bake 20-25 minutes or until cooked through.

2. In a large saucepan, combine vinegar, tomato paste, molasses, pepper sauce and remaining soy sauce; cook and stir over medium heat 3-5 minutes. Add meatballs; heat through, stirring gently to coat.

HOW TO PEEL GARLIC

- Place a head of garlic in one bowl and smash with the bottom of a similar-size bowl. You also can smash between two cutting boards. Have fun with it!

- Put the whole crushed bulbs in a hard-sided bowl with a similar-size bowl over the top. Metal is best, but you can use glass or even a firm plastic storage container with a lid. A jar also works, but it takes longer to shake.

- Shake vigorously for 10-15 seconds to separate the papery outer layers from the garlic cloves. The cloves will be peeled, and the skin can be easily discarded.

BUFFALO CHICKEN DIP

Buffalo wing sauce, cream cheese and ranch or blue cheese dressing make a great party dip. Everywhere I take it, people want the recipe.
—Belinda Gibson, Dry Ridge, KY

Start to Finish: 30 min. **Makes:** about 2 cups

1 package (8 ounces) cream cheese, softened
1 cup cooked chicken breast
½ cup Buffalo wing sauce
½ cup ranch or blue cheese salad dressing
2 cups shredded Colby-Monterey Jack cheese
French bread baguette slices, celery ribs or tortilla chips

1. Preheat oven to 350°. Spread cream cheese into an ungreased shallow 1-qt. baking dish. Layer with the chicken, wing sauce and salad dressing. Sprinkle with cheese.

2. Bake, uncovered, 20-25 minutes or until cheese is melted. Serve with baguette slices, celery ribs or chips.

✳ TEST KITCHEN TIP
Shredded rotisserie chicken works well. If you want an ooey-gooey top with very little browning, cover with foil when baking.

WHY YOU'LL LOVE IT...

"It's a favorite! I put everything in my slow cooker and cook on high 1-2 hours, then turn to low for serving. I use 2 cups rotisserie chicken, Frank's Red Hot sauce, 1½ cups cheese and ¼ cup ranch dressing with ¼ cup sour cream. I really like the creaminess the sour cream adds."

—NATTUMS, TASTEOFHOME.COM

CARAMELIZED HAM & SWISS BUNS

My next-door neighbor shared her version of this recipe with me. You can make it ahead and cook it quickly when company arrives. The combo of poppy seeds, ham and cheese, horseradish and brown sugar makes it simply delicious!
—Iris Weihemuller, Baxter, MN

Prep: 25 min. + chilling **Bake:** 30 min. **Makes:** 1 dozen

1 package (12 ounces) Hawaiian sweet rolls, split
½ cup horseradish sauce
12 slices deli ham
6 slices Swiss cheese, halved
½ cup butter, cubed
2 tablespoons finely chopped onion
2 tablespoons brown sugar
1 tablespoon spicy brown mustard
2 teaspoons poppy seeds
1½ teaspoons Worcestershire sauce
¼ teaspoon garlic powder

1. Spread the roll bottoms with horseradish sauce. Layer with ham and cheese; replace tops. Arrange rolls in a single layer in a greased 9-in. square baking pan.

2. In a small skillet, heat butter over medium-high heat. Add onion; cook and stir 1-2 minutes or until tender. Stir in remaining ingredients. Pour over rolls. Refrigerate, covered, several hours or overnight.

3. Preheat the oven to 350°. Bake, covered, 25 minutes. Bake, uncovered, 5-10 minutes longer or until rolls are golden brown.

HOW TO SPLIT BUNS

Don't waste time slicing buns one by one! Place one hand over the top of the buns to hold them steady. Using a serrated knife, gently cut horizontally. Carefully remove top half of the buns to separate. Place bottom half in baking dish.

✳
TEST KITCHEN TIP
Turn this sandwich into a Reuben! Swap corned beef or pastrami for the ham, add a layer of sauerkraut and substitute caraway seeds for poppy. Vegetarians coming for dinner? These buns can easily go meat-free by omitting the ham and doubling the cheese. We like Swiss and cheddar.

HOMEMADE GUACAMOLE

Nothing is better than freshly made guacamole when you're eating something spicy.
It's easy to whip together in a matter of minutes and quickly tames anything that's too hot.
—Joan Hallford, North Richland Hills, TX

Start to Finish: 10 min. **Make:** 2 cups

- 3 medium ripe avocados, peeled and cubed
- 1 garlic clove, minced
- ¼ to ½ teaspoon salt
- 2 medium tomatoes, seeded and chopped, optional
- 1 small onion, finely chopped
- ¼ cup mayonnaise, optional
- 1 to 2 tablespoons lime juice
- 1 tablespoon minced fresh cilantro

In a small or medium-size bowl, mash avocados with garlic and salt. Stir in remaining ingredients.

HOW TO PEEL AN AVOCADO

(Pictured bottom right, left to right)

- Cut into the ripe avocado (not too hard, not too squishy!) from stem to stern until you hit the seed. Repeat to cut the avocado into quarters.

- Twist to separate.

- Pull out the seed.

- Pull the skin back, just like a banana peel. Slice it or dice it as you like.

GARLIC-DILL DEVILED EGGS

*I like to experiment with my recipes and was pleasantly pleased with how
the fresh dill really perked up the flavor of these irresistible appetizers.*
—Kami Horch, Calais, ME

Prep: 20 min. + chilling **Makes:** 2 dozen

12 hard-boiled large eggs
⅔ cup mayonnaise
4 teaspoons dill pickle relish
2 teaspoons snipped fresh dill
2 teaspoons Dijon mustard
1 teaspoon coarsely ground pepper
¼ teaspoon garlic powder
⅛ teaspoon paprika or cayenne
   pepper

1. Cut eggs lengthwise in half. Remove yolks, reserving whites. In a bowl, mash yolks. Stir in all remaining ingredients except paprika. Spoon or pipe into the egg whites.

2. Refrigerate, covered, at least 30 minutes before serving. Sprinkle with paprika.

HOW TO MAKE CLASSIC DEVILED EGGS
(Pictured left, top to bottom)

Egg aficionados, rejoice! There are endless variations on this fun finger food. Begin by following these easy steps for basic deviled eggs, then season as desired.

- Hard cook the eggs. Not sure how? We'll tell you: Arrange in a single layer and add water to cover by 1 in. Bring to a rolling boil (constant bubbles), uncovered. Remove from the heat. Cover and let stand for 14-17 minutes.

- Drain the hot water and cover the eggs in cold water. Gently crack the shells and return to the cold water. Let stand 1 hour. After 1 hour, the shells will peel off easily.

- Trim a small part of the egg white from both sides to prevent wobbly eggs. Cut the eggs in half lengthwise and gently squeeze egg whites or use a small spoon to remove the yolk. Place the yolks in a bowl.

- Mash the yolks with the back of a fork until it's crumbly. Stir in the rest of the filling ingredients.

- Spoon or pipe filling into egg whites until slightly mounded.

- Spice it up! Garnish with paprika or your favorite herbs or spices.

LIKE 'EM HOT WINGS

These spicy chicken wings are wonderfully seasoned. They're an easy crowd-pleasing snack.
—Myra Innes, Auburn, KS

Prep: 10 min. **Bake:** 30 min. **Makes:** about 2 dozen

2½ pounds chicken wings
1 bottle (2 ounces) hot pepper sauce (about ¼ cup)
1 to 2 garlic cloves, minced
1½ teaspoons dried rosemary, crushed
1 teaspoon dried thyme
¼ teaspoon salt
¼ teaspoon pepper
Celery, carrot sticks and blue cheese salad dressing, optional

1. Cut chicken wings into three sections; discard wing tips. In a large resealable plastic bag, combine the hot pepper sauce, garlic and seasonings. Add wings; toss to evenly coat. Transfer to a well-greased 13x9-in. baking dish.

2. Bake the mixture, uncovered, at 425° for 30-40 minutes or until chicken juices run clear, turning every 10 minutes. Serve with celery, carrots and blue cheese dressing if desired.

Note: Uncooked chicken wing sections (wingettes) may be substituted for whole chicken wings.

HOW TO CUT CHICKEN WINGS

- With chicken wing on a cutting board, use a sharp knife to cut between the joint at the top of the tip end. Discard tips (or you can keep them for preparing chicken broth, if you want to be resourceful).

- Take remaining wing and cut between the joints. Proceed with recipe as directed.

BITE-SIZED
PIZZA!

LOADED PIZZA STRIPS

*Looking to add a dash of color to your appetizer mix? Topped with roasted peppers,
caramelized onions, beef and black olives, this popular pizza is as tasty as it is decorative on the table.*
—Margaret Pache, Mesa, AZ

Prep: 45 min. **Bake:** 20 min. **Makes:** 15 servings

- 2 tablespoons butter
- 1 teaspoon canola oil
- 1 large onion, thinly sliced
- 1 pound ground beef
- ½ teaspoon salt
- ⅛ teaspoon pepper
- 1 tablespoon cornmeal
- 1 tube (13.8 ounces) refrigerated pizza crust
- 1½ cups shredded part-skim mozzarella cheese
- 1 jar (7 ounces) roasted red peppers, drained and sliced
- 1 medium tomato, seeded and diced
- ½ cup sliced ripe olives

1. In a nonstick skillet, heat butter and oil; add onion. Cook and stir over low heat for 30-35 minutes or until onion is caramelized. In another skillet, cook beef over medium heat until no longer pink; drain. Sprinkle with salt and pepper; set aside.

2. Sprinkle cornmeal into a greased 13x9-in. baking pan. Press pizza dough into pan; prick dough with a fork. Bake at 400° for 10 minutes. Top with the beef, caramelized onion, cheese, red peppers, tomato and olives. Bake for 10-12 minutes longer or until cheese is melted. Cut into squares; serve warm.

GET THE BEST GROUND BEEF

- **Visit the butcher**

  Buy your ground beef from the meat counter, not the freezer section. The meat is usually ground fresh daily in the store. Look for meat that is pink with no gray spots.

- **Sirloin vs. chuck**

  Ground chuck has slightly more fat (85 percent) and is usually a little cheaper than ground sirloin. If you decide to use ground chuck, you'll probably want to drain the skillet to get rid of the extra grease.

BREADS, MUFFINS & ROLLS

Few things smell better than a loaf of bread fresh out of the oven. Here, we show you how to create that incredible experience right in your own kitchen. But it doesn't stop there: Follow the steps inside, and you'll be making crescent rolls, cast-iron corn bread and buttermilk biscuits in no time.

BUTTERMILK ANGEL BISCUITS

This recipe calls for a technique known as cutting in, which means rapidly breaking down shortening (or sometimes cold butter) with either a pastry blender or two knives.
—Carol Holladay, Danville, AL

Prep: 30 min. + standing **Bake:** 10 min. **Makes:** 2 dozen

2 packages (¼ ounce each) active dry yeast
¼ cup warm water (110° to 115°)
5¼ to 5½ cups self-rising flour
⅓ cup sugar
1 teaspoon baking soda
1 cup shortening
1¾ cups buttermilk

1. In a small bowl, dissolve yeast in warm water. In a large bowl, whisk 5¼ cups flour, sugar and baking soda. Cut in the shortening until mixture resembles coarse crumbs. Stir in buttermilk and yeast mixture to form a soft dough (dough will be sticky).

2. Turn onto a floured surface; knead gently 8-10 times, adding more flour if needed. Roll dough to ¾-in. thickness; cut with a floured 2½-in. biscuit cutter. Place 2 in. apart on greased baking sheets. Let stand at room temperature 20 minutes.

3. Preheat oven to 450°. Bake 8-12 minutes or until golden brown. Serve warm.

HOW TO MAKE BISCUITS
(Pictured bottom left, left to right)

- Turn dough onto a lightly floured surface and knead gently for as many times as the recipe directs. Be gentle! Overkneading will keep the dough from rising.

- Roll dough evenly to ¾-in. thickness.

- Cut with a floured biscuit cutter, using a straight downward motion; do not twist cutter. Twisting will make the layers stick together and the biscuits will not rise as high.

- Place biscuits on a greased baking sheet. Place 2 in. apart for biscuits with crusty sides or almost touching for softer sides.

✳
TEST KITCHEN TIP
To make sure active dry yeast (not quick-rise yeast) is alive and active, you may first want to proof it. Try this easy method:

Dissolve one package of yeast and 1 teaspoon sugar in ¼ cup warm water (110° to 115°). Let stand for 5 to 10 minutes. If the mixture foams up, the yeast mixture can be used because the yeast is doing its job. If it does not foam, throw the yeast away.

BASIC HOMEMADE BREAD

I enjoy the aroma of fresh homemade bread in my kitchen. Here's a simple yeast version that bakes up golden brown.
—Sandra Anderson, New York, NY

Prep: 20 min. + rising **Bake:** 30 min. + cooling
Makes: 2 loaves (16 slices each)

1 package (¼ ounce) active dry yeast
2¼ cups warm water (110° to 115°)
3 tablespoons sugar
1 tablespoon salt
2 tablespoons canola oil
6¼ to 6¾ cups all-purpose flour

1. In a large bowl, dissolve yeast in warm water. Add the sugar, salt, oil and 3 cups flour. Beat until smooth. Stir in enough remaining flour, ½ cup at a time, to form a soft dough.

2. Turn onto a floured surface; knead until smooth and elastic, 8-10 minutes. Place in a greased bowl, turning once to grease the top. Cover and let rise in a warm place until doubled, about 1½ hours.

3. Punch dough down. Turn onto a lightly floured surface; divide dough in half. Shape each into a loaf. Place in two greased 9x5-in. loaf pans. Cover and let rise until doubled, about 30-45 minutes.

4. Bake at 375° for 30-35 minutes or until golden brown and bread sounds hollow when tapped. Remove from pans to wire racks to cool.

HOW TO STORE HOMEMADE BREAD

- It's best to store bread at room temperature in a cool, dry place. In other words, don't let it see too much sun. To keep it soft, store in an airtight plastic bag. Stored this way, it will keep for 2-3 days.

- For longer storage, freeze bread for up to 3 months. Slice the bread before freezing, wrap tightly and remove slices as needed. Enjoy a sandwich on homemade bread whenever you want!

HOW TO WORK YEAST DOUGH

(Pictured above, left to right)

- Fold top of dough toward you. With your palms, push dough with a rolling motion away from you. Turn dough a quarter turn; repeat folding, kneading and turning until dough is smooth and elastic. Add flour to the surface as needed to avoid sticking. After kneading, place dough into a greased bowl, turning once to grease the top. Cover and let rise.

- Press two fingers ½ in. into the dough. If the dents remain, the dough has doubled in size.

- Punch dough down and place in greased pans. Cover with a towel and let rise in a warm (80°-85°), draft-free area; the oven and microwave are good options, but make sure they're turned off. Let dough rise until it has doubled.

CAST-IRON COMFORT

OVEN-FRIED CORN BREAD

This is an old Southern recipe that has been passed down from one generation to the next. It was originally called egg bread. The recipe requires a cast-iron skillet.
—Emory Doty, Jasper, GA

Prep: 20 min. **Bake:** 15 min. **Makes:** 8 servings

4 tablespoons canola oil, divided
1½ cups finely ground white cornmeal
¼ cup sugar
2 teaspoons baking powder
1 teaspoon baking soda
1 teaspoon salt
2 large eggs
2 cups buttermilk

1. Place 2 tablespoons oil in a 10-in. cast-iron skillet; place in oven. Preheat oven to 450°. Whisk together the cornmeal, sugar, baking powder, baking soda and salt. In another bowl, whisk together eggs, buttermilk and remaining oil. Add to cornmeal mixture; stir just until moistened.

2. Carefully remove hot skillet from oven. Add batter; bake until golden brown and a toothpick inserted in the center comes out clean, 15-20 minutes. Cut into wedges; serve warm.

SECRETS FOR SUCCESSFUL CORN BREAD

Here are some hints for making the best corn bread:

- Before using cornmeal, make sure it's fresh. It should have a slightly sweet smell. Rancid cornmeal will smell stale and musty. If it smells bad, toss it!

- To avoid overmixing, stir the batter by hand just until it is moistened. Lumps in the batter are normal and even desired. Give this method a try!

- Don't let the mixed batter stand before baking. Have the oven preheated and the skillet or pan ready to go.

- Corn bread tastes best fresh from the oven. If that's not possible, serve it as soon as you can after it's made for the most delicious results.

* See pages 77 and 155 for cast iron care tips.

BANANA NUT BREAD

This quick bread is a family favorite, so I always try to have ripe bananas on hand.
—Susan Jones, La Grange Park, IL

Prep: 10 min. **Bake:** 50 min. + cooling **Makes:** 1 loaf (16 slices)

¼ cup butter, softened
¾ cup sugar
2 large eggs
¾ cup mashed ripe banana (about 1 large)
½ cup sour cream
2¼ cups all-purpose flour
1 teaspoon ground cinnamon
¾ teaspoon baking soda
½ teaspoon salt
½ cup chopped walnuts
Additional walnuts, semisweet chocolate chips or coarse sugar, optional

1. Preheat oven to 350°. Beat butter and sugar until blended. Add eggs, one at a time, beating well after each addition. Stir in banana and sour cream. Whisk together the flour, cinnamon, baking soda and salt in a separate bowl. Add to butter mixture, stirring just until moistened. Fold in ½ cup walnuts.

2. Transfer to a greased 9x5-in. loaf pan. If desired, sprinkle with additional walnuts.

3. Bake until a toothpick inserted in center comes out clean, 50-60 minutes. Cool in pan 10 minutes before removing to a wire rack to cool.

Banana Chip Bread: Fold in 1 cup semisweet or white chocolate chips along with the chopped walnuts. Bake as directed.

HOW TO MAKE THE PERFECT BANANA BREAD

(Pictured above)

- Mash it! Use a potato masher to mash ripe bananas. Choose bananas that are yellow with lots of brown spots (the kind you'd normally think are too ripe to eat on their own).

- If desired, sprinkle batter with additional walnuts, chocolate chips or coarse sugar before baking. Yum!

MADE
WITH
♥

TENDER CRESCENT ROLLS

My family's holiday meal consists of different soups and breads. This is one of our favorites.
—Bonnie Myers, Callaway, NE

Prep: 45 min. + rising **Bake:** 10 min./batch **Makes:** 4 dozen

2 envelopes (¼ ounce each) active dry yeast
1 cup warm water (110° to 115°)
1 cup warm 2% milk (110° to 115°)
3 large eggs
½ cup sugar
6 tablespoons shortening
1 teaspoon salt
6½ to 7 cups all-purpose flour

*See page 12 for helpful tips on measuring ingredients.

1. In a small bowl, dissolve yeast in warm water. In a large bowl, combine milk, eggs, sugar, shortening, salt, yeast mixture and 3 cups flour; beat on medium speed 3 minutes until smooth. Stir in enough remaining flour to form a soft dough (dough will be sticky).

2. Turn the dough onto a floured surface; knead until smooth and elastic, 6-8 minutes. Place in a greased bowl, turning once to grease the top. Cover with a kitchen towel and let rise in a warm place until doubled, about 1 hour.

3. Punch down dough. Turn onto a lightly floured surface; divide into four portions. Roll each portion into a 12-in. circle; cut each into 12 wedges. Roll up wedges from the wide ends. Place 2 in. apart on greased baking sheets, point side down; curve to form crescents.

4. Cover with kitchen towels; let rise in a warm place until doubled, about 30 minutes. Preheat oven to 350°.

5. Bake 8-10 minutes or until golden brown. Remove from pans to wire racks; serve warm.

Herb Crescents: Add 1 tablespoon Italian seasoning with the sugar.

Cinnamon-Glazed Crescents: Prepare and bake rolls as directed. Heat 6 tablespoons butter in a small saucepan until golden brown. In a large bowl, whisk together 2 cups confectioners' sugar, 1½ teaspoons ground cinnamon, 2 teaspoons vanilla extract and browned butter until smooth. Whisk in 2-4 tablespoons of hot water to achieve spreading consistency. Brush over warm rolls.

Orange Crescents: Prepare the dough as directed. Combine 1 cup sugar and ¼ cup orange zest; sprinkle over dough circles. Cut, roll up and bake as directed. In a saucepan, bring 1½ cups sugar, 1 cup (8 ounces) sour cream, ½ cup butter and ¼ cup orange juice to a boil; cook and stir for 3 minutes. Pour over warm rolls.

CINNAMON DOUGHNUT MUFFINS

Back when my children were young, they loved these doughnut muffins
as after-school treats or with Sunday brunch. Adults love them, too!
—Sharon Pullen, Alvinston, ON

Prep: 15 min. **Bake:** 20 min. **Makes:** 10 standard-size muffins

1¾ cups all-purpose flour
1½ teaspoons baking powder
½ teaspoon salt
½ teaspoon ground nutmeg
¼ teaspoon ground cinnamon
¾ cups sugar
⅓ cup canola oil
1 large egg, lightly beaten
¾ cup milk
10 teaspoons seedless strawberry or other jam

TOPPING
¼ cup butter, melted
⅓ cup sugar
1 teaspoon ground cinnamon

1. In a large bowl, combine flour, baking powder, salt, nutmeg and cinnamon. In a small bowl, combine sugar, oil, egg and milk; stir into dry ingredients just until moistened.

2. Fill greased or paper-lined muffin cups half full; place 1 teaspoon jam on top. Cover jam with enough batter to fill muffin cups three-fourths full. Bake at 350° for 20-25 minutes or until a toothpick comes out clean.

3. Place melted butter in a small bowl; combine sugar and cinnamon in another bowl. Immediately after removing muffins from the oven, dip tops in butter, then in cinnamon-sugar. Serve warm.

JAMS, JELLIES & PRESERVES

What's the difference between jellies, jams and preserves? Glad you asked!

- **Jellies:** The fruit comes in the form of fruit juice. The finished product is smooth and clear.

- **Jams:** The fruit comes in the form of fruit pulp or crushed fruit. As a result, jam isn't as firm as jelly.

- **Preserves:** The fruit comes in the form of chunks in a syrup or a jam. The result is thick, and bits of fruit are visible.

HOW DO I MAKE...

BREAKFAST & BRUNCH

Rise and shine! Seize the day in a new way when you learn to make breakfast from scratch. Say goodbye to the days of relying on granola bars in the morning. And, go ahead, invite friends over for brunch! These recipes will absolutely blow them away.

VERY VANILLA FRENCH TOAST

These convenient French toast slices have creamy vanilla flavor from pudding mix, plus a hint of cinnamon. We like to top them with fresh berries.
—Linda Bernhagen, Plainfield, IL

Start to Finish: 10 min. **Makes:** 4 servings

1 cup milk
1 package (3 ounces) cook-and-serve vanilla pudding mix
1 large egg
½ teaspoon ground cinnamon
8 slices Texas toast
2 teaspoons butter

1. In a large bowl, whisk milk, pudding mix, egg and cinnamon for 2 minutes or until well blended. Dip toast in pudding mixture, coating both sides.

2. In a large skillet, melt butter over medium heat. Cook bread on both sides until golden brown.

TEST KITCHEN TIP
For a change of pace, try butterscotch pudding instead of vanilla.

WHY YOU'LL LOVE IT...

Best French Toast I have ever tasted! I've made it with both Texas toast bread and sliced French bread. Both were great! Now I make sure I always have a package of cook-and-serve vanilla pudding mix in my cupboard.

—JANENEMARIE, TASTEOFHOME.COM

BREAKFAST QUICHE

With two kinds of cheese, lots of crispy bacon and a dash of cayenne, this impressive quiche makes a big impression with brunch guests. It's the recipe my friends always ask for.
—Mark Clark, Twin Mountain, NH

Prep: 15 min. **Bake:** 30 min. + standing **Makes:** 6 servings

1¼ cups all-purpose flour
¼ teaspoon salt
½ cup cold butter
3 to 5 tablespoons ice water
FILLING
12 bacon strips, cooked and crumbled
½ cup shredded pepper jack or Monterey Jack cheese
½ cup shredded sharp cheddar cheese
⅓ cup finely chopped onion
4 large eggs
2 cups heavy whipping cream
¾ teaspoon salt
¼ teaspoon sugar
⅛ teaspoon cayenne pepper

1. Combine flour and salt; cut in butter until crumbly. Gradually add 3-5 tablespoons ice water, tossing with a fork until dough holds together when pressed. Wrap in plastic and refrigerate 1 hour.

2. Preheat oven to 450°. On a lightly floured surface, roll the dough to a ⅛-in.-thick circle; transfer to a 9-in. pie plate. Trim pastry to ½ in. beyond rim of plate; flute edge. Line unpricked pastry shell with a double thickness of heavy-duty foil. Bake 5 minutes; remove foil. Bake 5 minutes longer; remove from oven and cool on a wire rack. Reduce heat to 375°.

3. Sprinkle bacon, cheeses and onion over crust. Beat remaining ingredients in a bowl until blended; pour over top. Bake until a knife inserted in center comes out clean, 30-35 minutes. Let stand 10 minutes before cutting.

HOW TO MAKE QUICHE
(Pictured bottom left, left to right)

- Wrap the pie pastry in plastic and refrigerate before prebaking. In order for the butterfat to solidify, it needs a little time to chill.

- To prebake the crust, line pastry with foil; fill with dried beans or ceramic pie weights. Throw away dried beans after baking.

- There will be a little jiggle to the quiche when it comes out of the oven, but that's OK! The quiche is set if a knife comes out clean.

SWEET POTATO & ANDOUILLE HASH

When my husband was training for an athletic event, I looked for healthier recipes like these spicy sweet potatoes. Serve with a fried egg on the side for a filling meal.
—Marla Clark, Albuquerque, NM

Prep: 15 min. **Cook:** 25 min. **Makes:** 6 servings

2 tablespoons olive oil
½ pound fully cooked andouille sausage or fully cooked Spanish chorizo, finely chopped
4 cups finely chopped sweet potatoes (about 2 medium)
4 celery ribs, finely chopped
1 medium onion, finely chopped
4 garlic cloves, minced
½ teaspoon salt
¼ teaspoon pepper

1. In a Dutch oven, heat the oil over medium-high heat. Add sausage; cook and stir until browned.

2. Stir in remaining ingredients. Reduce heat to medium-low; cook, uncovered, 15-20 minutes or until potatoes are tender, stirring occasionally.

✳

TEST KITCHEN TIP
A Dutch oven is a heavy pan with a cover that can be used both on the stovetop and in the oven. A heavy fry pan or saucepan may be substituted in some cases, but if the recipe calls for the pan to go in the oven, make sure you use one that's oven-safe.

GOOD MORNING, SUNSHINE!

HOW TO MAKE CINNAMON ROLLS

(Pictured above, left to right)

- Roll one portion of the dough into an 18x12-in. rectangle. Spread with ¼ cup butter to within ½ in. of edges; sprinkle evenly with half of the brown sugar mixture. (The rest of the brown sugar mixture will be used for the other half of the dough.)

- Roll up jelly-roll style, starting with a long side; pinch seam to seal.

- Cut into 12 slices; repeat with the remaining ingredients.

OVERNIGHT CINNAMON ROLLS

I like to try different fun fillings in these soft rolls, and each one is packed with cinnamon flavor. They are definitely worth the overnight wait.
—Chris O'Connell, San Antonio, TX

Prep: 35 min. + rising **Bake:** 20 min. **Makes:** 2 dozen

- 2 packages (¼ ounce each) active dry yeast
- 1½ cups warm water (110° to 115°)
- 2 large eggs
- ½ cup butter, softened
- ½ cup sugar
- 2 teaspoons salt
- 5¾ to 6¼ cups all-purpose flour

CINNAMON FILLING
- 1 cup packed brown sugar
- 4 teaspoons ground cinnamon
- ½ cup softened butter, divided

GLAZE
- 2 cups confectioners' sugar
- ¼ cup half-and-half cream
- 2 teaspoons vanilla extract

1. In a small bowl, dissolve yeast in warm water. In a large bowl, combine eggs, butter, sugar, salt, yeast mixture and 3 cups flour; beat on medium speed until smooth. Stir in enough remaining flour to form a very soft dough (dough will be sticky). Do not knead. Cover with plastic wrap; refrigerate overnight.

2. In a small bowl, mix brown sugar and cinnamon. Turn dough onto a floured surface; divide dough in half. Roll one portion into an 18x12-in. rectangle. Spread with ¼ cup butter to within ½ in. of edges; sprinkle evenly with half of the brown sugar mixture.

3. Roll up jelly-roll style, starting with a long side; pinch seam to seal. Cut into 12 slices. Place in a greased 13x9-in. baking pan, cut side down. Repeat with remaining dough and filling.

4. Cover with kitchen towels; let rolls rise in a warm place until doubled, about 1 hour. Preheat oven to 375°.

5. Bake 20-25 minutes or until lightly browned. In a small bowl, mix the confectioners' sugar, cream and vanilla; spread over warm rolls.

Dark chocolate filling: Finely grate one 4-ounce bittersweet chocolate baking bar; gently stir in ½ cup sugar, 2 tablespoons baking cocoa and ½ teaspoon ground cinnamon. Sprinkle over softened butter in place of the brown sugar-cinnamon mixture.

Orange spice filling: Mix 1 cup packed brown sugar, 2 tablespoons orange zest, 2 teaspoons ground cinnamon, 1 teaspoon ground ginger and ½ teaspoon each ground cloves, ground cardamom and ground allspice until blended. Sprinkle over softened butter in place of the brown sugar-cinnamon mixture.

STUFFED HASH BROWNS

Since we met, my husband has regularly made me these hash browns with bacon, pepper jack and sour cream. We share them when we have guests, too.
—Annie Ciszak Pazar, Anchorage, AK

Prep: 15 min. **Cook:** 10 min./batch **Makes:** 4 servings

1 package (20 ounces) refrigerated shredded hash brown potatoes
¼ cup finely chopped onion
½ teaspoon salt
¼ teaspoon pepper
4 tablespoons olive oil, divided
½ cup pepper jack cheese
½ cup crumbled cooked bacon
½ cup sour cream
2 green onions, thinly sliced

1. In a large bowl, toss potatoes with onion, salt and pepper. In a small skillet, heat 2 teaspoons oil over medium heat. Add 1 cup potato mixture, pressing down to flatten with spatula. Cook, without stirring, 4-5 minutes or until the bottom is golden brown. Drizzle with 1 teaspoon oil; flip. Cook 4-5 minutes or until the bottom is golden brown, sprinkling with 2 tablespoons cheese and 2 tablespoons bacon during the last minute of cooking.

2. Fold hash browns in half; slide onto plate and keep warm. Repeat with remaining ingredients. Top with sour cream and green onions.

HOW TO COOK BACON IN THE OVEN
(Pictured bottom right, left to right)

- Place a wire rack in a 15x10-in. baking pan. Lightly spritz with cooking spray. Place bacon strips in a single layer on rack.

- Bake at 350° until bacon reaches desired texture, 20-30 minutes. Cook for a shorter time for soft bacon, longer for crisp.

- Use tongs to remove bacon strips from wire rack. Don't risk burning your fingers!

- Pour off grease into a heat-safe container before washing pan.

BRUNCH-
WORTHY
WOW!

AUNT EDITH'S BAKED PANCAKE

My aunt made a mighty breakfast that revolved around what we called the Big Pancake. I always enjoyed watching as she poured the batter into her huge iron skillet and then baked the confection to perfection in the oven.
—Marion Kirst, Troy, MI

Prep: 15 min. **Bake:** 20 min. **Makes:** 6 servings

3 large eggs
½ teaspoon salt
½ cup all-purpose flour
½ cup milk
2 tablespoons butter, softened
  Confectioners' sugar
  Lemon wedges

In a bowl, beat the eggs until very light. Add salt, flour and milk; beat well. Thoroughly rub bottom and sides of a 10-in. cast-iron or heavy skillet with butter. Pour batter into skillet. Bake at 450° for 15 minutes. Reduce heat to 350° and bake 5 minutes more or until set. Remove pancake from skillet and place on a large hot platter. Dust with confectioners' sugar and garnish with lemon. Serve immediately.

HOW TO REMOVE RUST FROM CAST IRON

- If your cast-iron skillet has only a small amount of rust, dampen a paper towel with cooking oil and wipe the rust away. Once the rust is gone, wipe the entire surface again with fresh oil and then reseason the pan. (Go to page 155 for reseasoning instructions.)

- To remove more than just a little rust, get the pan wet, add dish soap, then scrub with steel wool or a stiff scrubbing sponge. Work in small circles, focusing on the rustiest parts first, until you see the original black iron emerge. Rinse off the copper-brown suds in the sink.

- Make sure the skillet is clean by scrubbing again, this time with a softer soapy sponge. Dry the skillet with a clean dishrag. To dry the pan completely, place it on the stove and turn on the heat for a few minutes. When the pan is dry, reseason it.

PUMPKIN PIE-SPICED GRANOLA

*My husband says this granola with pumpkin and spices tastes like a bite
of real pumpkin pie, and it's a whole lot better for breakfast.*
—Sarah Ozimek, Oconomowoc, WI

Prep: 15 min. **Bake:** 40 min. + cooling **Makes:** 4 cups

4 cups old-fashioned oats
1 cup raw pumpkin seeds or pepitas
1 cup canned pumpkin
½ cup packed brown sugar
¼ cup honey
¼ cup canola oil
2 tablespoons water
2 teaspoons ground cinnamon
¾ teaspoon salt
¾ teaspoon ground ginger
¾ teaspoon ground nutmeg
¼ teaspoon ground cloves

1. Preheat oven to 325°. In a large bowl, combine oats and pumpkin seeds. In a small saucepan, whisk remaining ingredients; bring to a boil. Remove from heat. Pour over oat mixture; toss to coat.

2. Spread evenly into two greased 15x10-in. baking pans. Bake 40-50 minutes or until golden brown, stirring every 10 minutes. Cool completely on wire racks. Store in an airtight container.

WHY YOU'LL LOVE IT...

"I made a half-recipe but should have made the full amount! It's really good to snack on or paired with yogurt. Next time I'll probably mix in some dried cranberries or cherries after it's done baking."

—CATGURL006, TASTEOFHOME.COM

HOW TO CRACK AN EGG ON THE COUNTERTOP

(Pictured above)

- Imagine the egg is standing upright. The middle or equator of the egg, where it might wear a belt, is its weakest point. Target this area when cracking. Gently but firmly grasp the egg. Rap it against the countertop so its equator lands squarely against the surface. Be calm and confident. It's better to give it one sharp tap than several gentle, tentative ones. Cracking an egg too hard can crush the shell, making it nearly inevitable you'll wind up with tiny shell fragments. Not fun.

- Once the shell breaks, work the opening to release the egg. Use your thumbs to press slightly inward and separate the shell, then pour the contents of the shell into a bowl.

WHY NOT CRACK EGGS ON THE RIM OF A BOWL?

Most of us instinctively crack eggs on the rim of a bowl. However, this method increases the risk of shell fragments falling in. It makes sense: If you crack an egg right over the bowl and the shell shatters—as they sometimes do—the pieces will fall in. Cracking eggs on a flat surface, such as a countertop, keeps the membrane intact and helps hold the small shell pieces in place while the egg falls into the bowl.

CREAM CHEESE & CHIVE OMELET

The first bite of creamy filling lets you know this isn't any ordinary omelet. If you make it once, I suspect you'll be fixing it often.
—Anne Troise, Manalapan, NJ

Start to Finish: 15 min. **Makes:** 2 servings

1 tablespoon olive oil
4 large eggs
2 tablespoons minced chives
2 tablespoons water
⅛ teaspoon salt
⅛ teaspoon pepper
2 ounces cream cheese, cubed
Salsa

1. In a large nonstick skillet, heat oil over medium-high heat. Whisk the eggs, chives, water, salt and pepper. Add egg mixture to skillet (mixture should set immediately at edges).

2. As eggs set, push cooked edges toward the center, letting uncooked portion flow underneath. When the eggs are set, sprinkle cream cheese on one side; fold other side over filling. Slide omelet onto a plate; cut in half. Serve with salsa.

✳

TEST KITCHEN TIP
Did you drop eggshell into your mixture by accident? Fish out the fragments with one of the shell halves instead of your finger—shell tends to stick to shell.

HOW DO I MAKE...

SOUPS, SALADS & SANDWICHES

Take your sandwiches, salads and soups from blah to brilliant. Let fresh veggies shine in salads, feel better with homemade chicken noodle soup and make comfort food fast with the ultimate grilled cheese. Learn it all here!

PULLED CHICKEN SANDWICHES

I'm a Southern girl, raised with the love of barbecue built into my DNA.
This slow cooker recipe allows me to enjoy the flavors I grew up eating.
—Heidi Mulholland, Cumming, GA

Prep: 20 min. **Cook:** 4 hours **Makes:** 6 servings

1 medium onion, finely chopped
1 can (6 ounces) tomato paste
¼ cup reduced-sodium chicken broth
2 tablespoons brown sugar
1 tablespoon cider vinegar
1 tablespoon yellow mustard
1 tablespoon Worcestershire sauce
2 garlic cloves, minced
2 teaspoons chili powder
¾ teaspoon salt
⅛ teaspoon cayenne pepper
1½ pounds boneless skinless chicken breasts
6 whole wheat hamburger buns, split

1. In a small bowl, mix the first eleven ingredients. Place chicken in a 3-qt. slow cooker. Pour sauce over top.

2. Cook, covered, on low 4-5 hours or until chicken is tender. Remove chicken; cool slightly. Shred meat with two forks. Return to slow cooker; heat through. Serve in buns.

To freeze: Freeze cooled chicken mixture in freezer containers. To use, partially thaw in refrigerator overnight. Heat through in a saucepan, stirring occasionally and adding a little broth if necessary.

* Turn to page 256 for more recipes that are slow cooker-friendly!

HOW TO REMOVE BEET SKIN

(Pictured left, top to bottom)

- On a cutting board, cut the beet greens to 1 inch and cut off the tail (root end).

- Place trimmed beets in a Dutch oven or baking dish; add enough water to cover, and then cook according to recipe directions.

- With a slotted spoon, carefully remove beets to a bowl of cold water.

- When beets are cool enough to handle, trim off what's left of the stem. Grab a couple of paper towels and hold one in each hand. Pick up a beet with both hands, hold firmly, and twist your hands in opposite directions. The skin will slide right off and your hands will stay clean.

BERRY-BEET SALAD

Here's a delightfully different salad that balances the earthy flavor of beets with the natural sweetness of berries. If you prefer, substitute crumbled feta for the goat cheese.
—Amy Lyons, Mounds View, MN

Prep: 20 min. **Bake:** 30 min. + cooling **Makes:** 4 servings

1 each fresh red and golden beets
¼ cup balsamic vinegar
2 tablespoons walnut oil
1 teaspoon honey
    Dash salt
    Dash pepper
½ cup sliced fresh strawberries
½ cup fresh raspberries
½ cup fresh blackberries
3 tablespoons chopped walnuts,
    toasted
1 shallot, thinly sliced
4 cups torn mixed salad greens
1 ounce fresh goat cheese,
    crumbled
1 tablespoon fresh basil, thinly sliced

1. Place the beets in an 8-in. square baking dish; add 1 in. of water. Cover and bake at 400° for 30-40 minutes or until tender.

2. Meanwhile, in a small bowl, whisk the vinegar, oil, honey, salt and pepper; set aside. Cool the beets; peel and cut into thin slices.

3. In a large bowl, combine the beets, berries, walnuts and shallot. Pour dressing over beet mixture and toss gently to coat. Divide salad greens among four serving plates. Top with the beet mixture; sprinkle with cheese and basil.

ROASTED POTATO & GREEN BEAN SALAD

I made this salad to take advantage of seasonal potatoes, onions and green beans.
It's a perfect twist on the tangy German potato salad my mom used to make.
—Blair Lonergan, Rochelle, VA

Prep: 15 min. **Bake:** 25 min. **Makes:** 7 servings

- 6 medium red potatoes, cut into 1-inch cubes
- 1 large red onion, cut into 1-inch pieces
- ¼ pound fresh green beans, trimmed and halved
- 2 tablespoons olive oil
- 8 bacon strips, cooked and crumbled

VINAIGRETTE
- 2 tablespoons cider vinegar
- 1 tablespoon minced fresh thyme or 1 teaspoon dried thyme
- 1 tablespoon lemon juice
- 1 tablespoon Dijon mustard
- ½ teaspoon salt
- ¼ teaspoon pepper
- ¼ cup olive oil

1. Preheat oven to 425°. Place potatoes, onion and green beans in a greased 15x10x1-in. baking pan. Drizzle with oil; toss to coat.

2. Roast 25-30 minutes or until tender, stirring twice. Transfer to a large bowl; add bacon. In a small bowl, whisk first six vinaigrette ingredients. Gradually whisk in oil until blended. Pour over potato mixture; toss to coat. Serve mixture warm.

HOW TO TRIM GREEN BEANS

- Before you get cooking, remove the tough, withered ends from the beans. You can do this with a knife or scissors—but your hands work just as well. *Psst!* This is a great task for getting the kids involved.

- If you prefer to just cut and be done, simply line up the ends of the beans. Then, using a chef's knife, slice several at a time.

TAKEOUT
FAKE OUT!

CHEESY BROCCOLI SOUP IN A BREAD BOWL

This creamy, cheesy broccoli soup tastes just like Panera! My family requests it all the time. You can even make your own homemade bread bowls, if you want.
—Rachel Preus, Marshall, MI

Prep: 5 min. **Cook:** 30 min. **Makes:** 6 servings

¼ cup butter, cubed
½ cup chopped onion
2 garlic cloves, minced
4 cups fresh broccoli florets (about 8 ounces)
1 large carrot, finely chopped
3 cups chicken stock
2 cups half-and-half cream
2 bay leaves
½ teaspoon salt
¼ teaspoon ground nutmeg
¼ teaspoon pepper
¼ cup cornstarch
¼ cup water or additional chicken stock
2½ cups shredded cheddar cheese
6 small round bread loaves (about 8 ounces each)

1. In a 6-qt. stockpot, heat butter over medium heat; saute onion and garlic until tender, 6-8 minutes. Stir in broccoli, carrot, stock, cream and seasonings; bring to a boil. Simmer, uncovered, until vegetables are tender, 10-12 minutes.

2. Mix cornstarch and water until smooth; stir into soup. Bring to a boil, stirring occasionally; cook and stir until thickened, 1-2 minutes. Remove bay leaves. Stir in cheese until melted.

3. Cut a slice off the top of each bread loaf; hollow out the bottoms, leaving ¼-in.-thick shells (save removed bread for another use). Fill with soup just before serving.

HOW TO MAKE A BREAD BOWL

- Cut a thin slice off the top of the bread loaf.

- Hollow out the bottom of the loaf, leaving a ¼-in.-thick shell. Add soup, stew or chili when ready to serve.

✱
TEST KITCHEN TIP
These bowls make for a hearty meal on their own but are also delicious as appetizers. Smaller, sturdy breads such as hard rolls are a good choice for a pre-dinner portion.

THE ULTIMATE GRILLED CHEESE

These gooey grilled cheese sandwiches, subtly seasoned with garlic, taste great for lunch with sliced apples. To save time, I soften the cream cheese in the microwave, then blend it with the rest of the ingredients in the same bowl. That makes cleanup a breeze.

—Kathy Norris, Streator, IL

Start to Finish: 15 min. **Makes:** 5 servings

3 ounces cream cheese, softened
¾ cup mayonnaise
1 cup shredded part-skim mozzarella cheese
1 cup shredded cheddar cheese
½ teaspoon garlic powder
⅛ teaspoon seasoned salt
10 slices Italian bread (½ inch thick)
2 tablespoons butter, softened

1. In a large bowl, beat the cream cheese and mayonnaise until smooth. Stir in the cheeses, garlic powder and seasoned salt. Spread five slices of bread with cheese mixture, about ⅓ cup on each. Top with remaining bread.

2. Butter the outsides of sandwiches. In a skillet over medium heat, toast sandwiches for 4-5 minutes on each side or until bread is lightly browned and cheese is melted.

WHY YOU'LL LOVE IT...

"I've added chunks of cooked chicken to this cheese mixture and spread it on tortilla shells for great quesadillas. My college-aged kids still request them!"

—BJS1967, TASTEOFHOME.COM

SHRIMP AVOCADO SALAD

This salad can be served as a cool and satisfying dinner or lunch.
The delicious taste of avocados mixed with the crisp shrimp salad is heavenly.
—Teri Rasey, Cadillac, MI

Prep: 25 min. + chilling **Makes:** 6 servings

- 1 pound peeled and deveined cooked shrimp, coarsely chopped
- 2 plum tomatoes, seeded and chopped
- 2 green onions, chopped
- ¼ cup finely chopped red onion
- 1 jalapeno pepper, seeded and minced
- 1 serrano pepper, seeded and minced
- 2 tablespoons minced fresh cilantro
- 2 tablespoons lime juice
- 2 tablespoons seasoned rice vinegar
- 2 tablespoons olive oil
- 1 teaspoon adobo seasoning
- 3 medium ripe avocados, peeled and cubed
  Bibb lettuce leaves
  Lime wedges

1. Place first seven ingredients in a large bowl. Mix lime juice, vinegar, oil and adobo seasoning; stir into shrimp mixture. Refrigerate, covered, to allow flavors to blend, about 1 hour.

2. To serve, gently stir in avocados. Serve over lettuce leaves. Serve with lime wedges.

Note: Wear disposable gloves when cutting hot peppers; the oils can burn skin. Avoid touching your face.

✳
TEST KITCHEN TIP
You can buy shrimp that are already deveined and peeled, but if you need to do it yourself, here's how:

To peel, start by the head area of the shrimp. Pull legs and first section of shell to one side. Continue pulling shell up around the top and to other side. Pull off shell by tail if desired.

Remove the black vein running down the back of the shrimp by making a shallow slit with a paring knife along the back from the head area to the tail.

Rinse each shrimp under cold water to remove the vein.

* See page 42 for instructions on peeling avocados.

HOMEY CHICKEN NOODLE SOUP

Chicken noodle soup brings back warm childhood memories. This revamped version adds a healthy twist with kale. It's a favorite at my house, especially after a cool day spent outside.
—Cynthia LaFourcade, Salmon, ID

Prep: 15 min. **Cook:** 50 min. **Makes:** 6 servings (about 2½ quarts)

¼ cup butter, cubed
1 medium onion, chopped
2 celery ribs, chopped
2 medium carrots, chopped
¾ cup coarsely chopped fresh mushrooms
1 garlic clove, minced
¼ cup all-purpose flour
1½ teaspoons dried basil
½ teaspoon salt
2 cartons (32 ounces each) reduced-sodium chicken broth
1 package (12 ounces) frozen home-style egg noodles
4 cups chopped fresh kale
2 cups shredded cooked chicken

1. In a Dutch oven, heat butter over medium heat. Add onion, celery, carrots and mushrooms; cook and stir 8-10 minutes or until vegetables are crisp-tender. Add minced garlic; cook 1 minute longer.

2. Stir in flour, dried basil and salt until blended; gradually stir in broth. Bring to a boil. Reduce heat; simmer, covered, 10 minutes.

3. Return to a boil; add noodles. Reduce the heat; simmer, covered, 15 minutes. Stir in kale and chicken; cook, covered, 6-8 minutes longer or until kale and noodles are tender.

To freeze: Freeze cooled soup in freezer containers. To use, partially thaw in refrigerator overnight. Heat soup through in a saucepan, stirring occasionally and adding a little broth if necessary.

HOW TO TRIM KALE

If your kale is thin and tender, just snip off the bottom of the stems with kitchen shears. If the stems are thicker, you'll need to remove them from the leaves completely. Place each leaf on a cutting board, fold in half lengthwise and use a knife to carefully slice the stem away from the leaf.

✳

TEST KITCHEN TIP
In a rush? Grab a rotisserie chicken on the way home and shred the meat to throw into this soup.

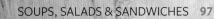

HOW TO MAKE
CHOPPED SALAD

(Pictured above, left to right)

- This recipe involves a decent amount of prep work—but don't let that intimidate you. Cut the peppers lengthwise into matchsticks, then cut horizontally into small squares (about ½ inch in size). Chop the tomato into pieces of a similar size as the chopped pepper—no need to be exact. Chop the cucumber, zucchini and green onions to roughly the same size and shape. Toss the vegetables and the minced parsley into a large bowl.

- In a small bowl, whisk the olive oil, vinegar, sugar, salt and pepper. If you're serving the salad right away, drizzle the dressing over the veggie mix. If making this recipe in advance (or if your guests are fussy about dressing), keep the vinaigrette in a small mason jar on the side. Give it a quick shake before using.

- Toss vegetables with dressing. Add diced avocado and stir gently to incorporate.

FIESTA CHOPPED SALAD

We serve this colorful garden feast when we find vegetables bursting with flavor. The dressing makes this fresh salad a welcome companion for most any entree.
—Merwyn Garbini, Tucson, AZ

Start to Finish: 30 min. **Makes:** 8 servings

1 medium sweet red pepper, chopped
1 medium sweet yellow pepper, chopped
1 medium tomato, seeded and chopped
1 medium cucumber, seeded and chopped
1 small zucchini, chopped
2 green onions, chopped
2 tablespoons minced fresh parsley
2 tablespoons olive oil
1 tablespoon red wine vinegar
½ teaspoon sugar
¼ teaspoon salt
¼ teaspoon pepper
1 large ripe avocado, peeled and chopped
1 tablespoon lemon juice

In a large bowl, combine the first seven ingredients. In a small bowl, whisk the oil, vinegar, sugar, salt and pepper. Drizzle over the vegetables and toss to coat. Toss avocado with lemon juice; gently fold into salad. Serve with a slotted spoon.

＊

TEST KITCHEN TIP
Wondering what *minced* means? Minced pieces should be as small as you can make 'em. Work the knife in a back-and-forth rocking motion. Because the pieces will be tiny, they don't have to be uniform.

WEEKNIGHT TACO SOUP

This soup turned out delicious on the first try. For a heartier meal, try adding cooked ground beef or cubed stew meat that's been dredged in seasoned flour and browned.
—Amanda Swartz, Goderich, ON

Start to Finish: 30 min. **Makes:** 6 servings (2½ quarts)

1 tablespoon canola oil
1 large onion, chopped
1 medium sweet red pepper, chopped
1 medium green pepper, chopped
1 can (28 ounces) diced tomatoes, undrained
3 cups vegetable broth
1 can (15 ounces) pinto beans, rinsed and drained
1½ cups frozen corn
1 envelope taco seasoning
¼ teaspoon salt
¼ teaspoon pepper
1 package (8.8 ounces) ready-to-serve long grain rice
1 cup (8 ounces) sour cream
  Optional toppings: shredded cheddar cheese, crushed tortilla chips and additional sour cream

1. In a Dutch oven, heat oil over medium heat. Add onion and peppers; cook and stir 3-5 minutes or until crisp-tender.

2. Add the tomatoes, broth, beans, corn, taco seasoning, salt and pepper; bring to a boil. Reduce heat; simmer, uncovered, 10-15 minutes or until the vegetables are tender. Reduce heat. Stir in rice and sour cream; heat through. Serve with toppings as desired.

To freeze: Freeze cooled soup in freezer containers. To use, partially thaw in refrigerator overnight. Heat soup through in a saucepan, stirring occasionally and adding a little broth if necessary.

WHY YOU'LL LOVE IT...

"Yummy! This taco soup is the best. I added 4 cups of vegetable broth instead of 3. I did not add the sour cream but decided to serve it on the side along with the cheese. Will definitely make it again."

—SLAMOTHE, TASTEOFHOME.COM

TACO
TUESDAY
WITH A
TWIST!

BACON AVOCADO SALAD

Everyone in my family loves this summery salad—even the younger kids! I serve it at pretty much every get-together I host, and at this point, the recipe's been shared too many times to count.
—Noreen McCormick Danek, Cromwell, CT

Start to Finish: 25 min. **Makes:** 10 servings

¾ cup extra virgin olive oil
¼ cup red wine vinegar
4 teaspoons sugar
2 garlic cloves, minced
1 teaspoon salt
1 teaspoon Dijon mustard

SALAD
1 bunch romaine, chopped (about 12 cups)
¾ pound bacon strips, cooked and crumbled
3 medium tomatoes, chopped
1 medium red onion, halved and thinly sliced
3 medium ripe avocados, peeled and cubed
2 tablespoons lemon juice
1 cup crumbled Gorgonzola or feta cheese

1. Place first six ingredients in a jar with a tight-fitting lid; shake well until blended. Refrigerate until serving.

2. In a large bowl, combine romaine, bacon, tomatoes and onion. Toss avocados with lemon juice and add to salad. Sprinkle with cheese. Serve with dressing, shaking to blend again if needed.

* See page 74 for how to cook bacon in the oven.

QUICK & EASY TURKEY SLOPPY JOES

When we were first married, I found this simple recipe and adjusted it to our tastes. The fresh bell pepper and red onion give it wonderful flavor.
—Kallee Twiner, Maryville, TN

Start to Finish: 30 min. **Makes:** 8 servings

1 pound lean ground turkey
1 large red onion, chopped
1 large green pepper, chopped
1 can (8 ounces) tomato sauce
½ cup barbecue sauce
1 teaspoon dried oregano
1 teaspoon ground cumin
1 teaspoon chili powder
¼ teaspoon salt
8 hamburger buns, split

1. In a large skillet, cook turkey, onion and green pepper over medium heat 6-8 minutes or until turkey is no longer pink and vegetables are tender, breaking up turkey into crumbles.

2. Stir in tomato sauce, barbecue sauce and seasonings. Bring to a boil. Reduce heat; simmer, uncovered, 10 minutes, to allow the flavors to blend, stirring occasionally. Serve on buns.

HOW LONG DO LEFTOVERS LAST?

Wondering how long cooked chicken or a leftover slice of pizza lasts in the fridge? Look no further than this handy list:

Refrigerator Storage

- **The following foods will keep for only 1-2 days in the refrigerator:**
  - Fresh (raw) ground meats and stew meats
  - Gravy and meat broth
  - Fresh poultry and fresh fish
  - Shrimp, scallops, crayfish and squid
  - Shucked clams, mussels and oysters

- **The following foods will keep for 3-4 days in the refrigerator:**
  - Fully cooked ham slices
  - Cooked meat and meat casseroles
  - Cooked chicken and chicken casseroles
  - Pizza
  - Cooked fish and shellfish

- **The following items will keep for up to 5 days in the refrigerator:**
  - Opened packages of lunch or deli meats
  - Fully cooked ham portions
  - Fresh meat steaks, chops and roasts

- **The following foods have longer refrigerator storage times:**
  - Fresh eggs in shells = 3-5 weeks
  - Hard-cooked eggs = 1 week
  - Commercial mayonnaise after opening = 2 months
  - Opened hard cheese (such as cheddar or Swiss) = 3-4 weeks
  - Soft cheese (such as Brie or feta); cottage cheese; ricotta and milk = 1 week
  - Yogurt = 7-14 days

- **When in doubt, throw it out:** If you lose track of how long a food has been in the refrigerator, it's best to not risk eating it. (To avoid this problem in the future, label and date your leftovers before refrigerating.)

- **Store food wisely:** For best storage, it's wise to divvy up hot leftovers into smaller portions, then place in shallow dishes to cool quickly. Wait until steam has stopped rising from the food before chilling, so the steam won't heat up your fridge. Choose strong food storage containers that are clean and in good condition, and opt for covered containers—they're always a better choice than uncovered bowls. Never store food in the can it came in.

- **Don't leave dishes at room temp for too long:** Food that sits out on the counter for too long can start growing harmful bacteria. Try to get food in the refrigerator within 2 hours after it's cooked (or sooner, if it's cooled enough). If food has been left out for longer than 2 hours, it may be unsafe. Err on the safe side and toss.

HOW DO I MAKE...

SIDE DISHES

It's OK…we won't spill the beans if your current go-to side is a bag of chips. But let's take the next step together by making savory, simple recipes to accompany any main dish.

CHEESY CHEDDAR BROCCOLI CASSEROLE

People who don't even like broccoli beg me to make this comforting recipe. It's similar to a classic green bean casserole, but the melted cheese puts it over the top.
—Elaine Hubbard, Pocono Lake, PA

Prep: 15 min. **Bake:** 35 min. **Makes:** 8 servings

1 can (10¾ ounces) condensed cream of mushroom soup, undiluted
1 cup (8 ounces) sour cream
1½ cups shredded sharp cheddar cheese, divided
1 can (6 ounces) french-fried onions, divided
2 packages (16 ounces each) frozen broccoli florets, thawed

1. Preheat oven to 325°. In a large saucepan, combine the soup, sour cream, 1 cup cheese and 1¼ cups onions; heat through over medium heat, stirring until blended, 4-5 minutes. Stir in broccoli. Transfer to a greased 2-qt. baking dish.

2. Bake, uncovered, until bubbly, 25-30 minutes. Sprinkle with the remaining cheese and onions. Bake until cheese is melted, 10-15 minutes.

WHY YOU'LL LOVE IT...

"This was really good! Great alternative to green bean casserole."
—MJLOUK, TASTEOFHOME.COM

SKILLET SCALLOPED POTATOES

Our garden is a big inspiration when I'm cooking. This recipe turns the product of my husband's potato patch into a side dish we want to eat at every meal.
—Lori Daniels, Beverly, WV

Start to Finish: 30 min. **Makes:** 4 servings

1 tablespoon butter
1 pound small red potatoes, thinly sliced (about 3 cups)
1 tablespoon dried minced onion
¾ cup chicken broth
½ cup half-and-half cream
¾ teaspoon salt
¼ teaspoon pepper
1 cup shredded cheddar cheese

1. In a large nonstick skillet, heat butter over medium heat. Add potatoes and onion; cook and stir for 5 minutes.

2. Stir in broth, cream, salt and pepper. Bring to a boil. Reduce heat; simmer, covered, for 10-12 minutes or until potatoes are tender. Sprinkle with cheese; cook, covered, 2-3 minutes longer or until cheese is melted.

❋
TEST KITCHEN TIP
Red potatoes are popular for boiling and steaming. They have a thin skin, and the pigment makes the potato a colorful choice for salads.

RAINBOW HASH

To get my family to eat outside of their comfort zone, I use lots of color.
This happy hash combines sweet potato, carrot, purple potato and kale.
—Courtney Stultz, Weir, KS

....

Start to Finish: 30 min. **Makes:** 2 servings

2 tablespoons olive or coconut oil
1 medium sweet potato, peeled and cubed
1 medium purple potato, peeled and cubed
1 large carrot, peeled and cubed
½ teaspoon dried oregano
½ teaspoon dried basil
½ teaspoon sea salt
½ teaspoon pepper
2 cups fresh kale or spinach, coarsely chopped
1 small garlic clove, minced

In a large skillet, heat oil over medium heat. Cook and stir potatoes, carrot and seasonings until vegetables are tender, 10-12 minutes. Add kale and garlic; continue cooking until the vegetables are lightly browned and kale is tender, 2-4 minutes.

* Turn to page 96 to learn about trimming kale.

HOW TO PEEL A CARROT

(Pictured right, top to bottom)

- Hold carrot at a 45-degree angle on a cutting board. Hold the peeler in your dominant hand. Peel just the bottom half first so your carrot-holding hand stays out of the way.

- Start the vegetable peeler at the middle of the carrot and peel downward toward the cutting board; when you reach the end of the carrot, rotate it slightly and switch directions (peel back upward). Stop at the center of the carrot. Rotate the carrot and peel another stripe. Repeat until the bottom half is peeled; the top half of the carrot will remain unpeeled as you peel the bottom.

- Flip the carrot so you're holding the peeled end. Rest the unpeeled end against the cutting board at a 45-degree angle. Repeat the steps above, peeling down and then up, rotating the carrot until it's completely peeled.

- With some practice, this method should be simple and efficient. You'll get faster as you become more familiar with the movement. (Many people prefer to peel downward only, and that's also fine!) This method works well for many vegetables, particularly those with a long, thin shape, such as parsnips, cucumbers and zucchini.

BRANDY-GLAZED CARROTS

I found this recipe about 10 years ago in an old cookbook I got at a thrift store. I changed the sugar it called for to honey. Once these carrots are glazed, not only are they delicious, but they look pretty, too.
—Tammy Landry, Saucier, MS

Start to Finish: 30 min. **Makes:** 12 servings (¾ cup each)

- 3 **pounds fresh baby carrots**
- ½ **cup butter, cubed**
- ½ **cup honey**
- ¼ **cup brandy**
- ¼ **cup minced fresh parsley**
- ½ **teaspoon salt**
- ¼ **teaspoon pepper**

In a large skillet, bring ½ in. of water to a boil. Add carrots. Cover and cook for 5-9 minutes or until crisp-tender. Drain and set aside. In the same skillet, cook butter and honey over medium heat until butter is melted. Remove from heat; stir in brandy. Bring to a boil; cook until liquid is reduced to about ½ cup. Add the carrots, parsley, salt and pepper; heat through.

WHY YOU'LL LOVE IT...

"I was very pleased with how easy this dish was to make but also surprised by how great it tasted. If you enjoy a recipe that allows you to indulge in the fresh taste of baby carrots, then this will be a hit at the dinner table."

—TAMMYTEE2, TASTEOFHOME.COM

PASTA WITH ASPARAGUS

I discovered this zippy, tempting dish at a get-together with friends. The garlic, asparagus, Parmesan cheese and red pepper flakes create an irresistible taste combo.
—Jean Fisher, Redlands, CA

Start to Finish: 20 min. **Makes:** 4-6 servings

5 garlic cloves, minced
¼ to ½ teaspoon crushed red pepper flakes
2 to 3 dashes hot pepper sauce
¼ cup olive oil
1 tablespoon butter
1 pound fresh asparagus, cut into 1½-inch pieces
Salt to taste
¼ teaspoon pepper
¼ cup shredded Parmesan cheese
½ pound mostaccioli or elbow macaroni, cooked and drained

In a large skillet, cook the garlic, red pepper flakes and hot pepper sauce in oil and butter for 1 minute. Add the asparagus, salt and pepper; saute until the asparagus is crisp-tender, about 8-10 minutes. Stir in the cheese. Pour over hot pasta and toss to coat. Serve immediately.

✳

TEST KITCHEN TIP
Asparagus is in season from February through late June, with its peak in the spring. Choose small, straight stalks with tightly closed, compact tips. Spears should be smooth and round. To store, refrigerate unwashed green asparagus in a sealed plastic bag for up to 4 days (or 2 days for white asparagus).

HOW TO PREP ASPARAGUS

(Pictured above, left to right)

- Rinse asparagus stalks well in cold water. The tender stalk should easily break from the tough white portion when gently bent. If not, cut off the white portion.

- If the tips are particularly large, use a knife to scrape off some of the scales.

- If the stalks are large, use a vegetable peeler to gently remove the tough area of the stalk from just below the tip to the end.

SERVE A CROWD!

PATIO PINTOS

Any time Mom had the gang over for dinner, she made these pinto beans.
Once, she made a batch for my cousin's birthday, and he ate the entire thing.
—Joan Hallford, North Richland Hills, TX

Prep: 25 min. **Bake:** 1 hour **Makes:** 10 servings

½ pound bacon strips, chopped
1 large onion, chopped
2 garlic cloves, minced
6 cans (15 ounces each) pinto beans, rinsed and drained
4 cans (8 ounces each) tomato sauce
2 cans (4 ounces each) chopped green chilies
⅓ cup packed brown sugar
1 teaspoon chili powder
¾ teaspoon salt
½ teaspoon dried oregano
¼ teaspoon pepper

1. Preheat oven to 350°. In a Dutch oven, cook bacon over medium heat until crisp, stirring occasionally. Remove with a slotted spoon; drain on paper towels. Discard the drippings, reserving 2 tablespoons in pan.

2. Add onion to drippings; cook and stir over medium heat 6-8 minutes or until tender. Add garlic; cook 1 minute longer. Stir in beans, tomato sauce, green chilies, brown sugar and all seasonings. Sprinkle top with bacon. Bake, covered, 60-70 minutes or until heated through.

To freeze: Freeze cooled bean mixture in freezer containers. To use, partially thaw in refrigerator overnight. Heat beans through in a saucepan, stirring occasionally and adding a little water if necessary.

✻
TEST KITCHEN TIP
Out of fresh garlic? Grab the garlic powder, and substitute ¼ teaspoon of powder for each clove called for in a recipe.

ROASTED VEGETABLES WITH SAGE

When I can't decide which veggie to serve, I roast a variety at once!
—Betty Fulks, Onia, AR

Prep: 20 min. **Bake:** 35 min. **Makes:** 8 servings

5 cups cubed peeled butternut squash
½ pound fingerling potatoes (about 2 cups)
1 cup fresh Brussels sprouts, halved
1 cup fresh baby carrots
3 tablespoons butter
1 tablespoon minced fresh sage or 1 teaspoon dried sage leaves
1 garlic clove, minced
½ teaspoon salt

1. Preheat oven to 425°. Place vegetables in a large bowl. In a microwave, melt butter; stir in remaining ingredients. Add to vegetables and toss to coat.

2. Transfer to a greased 15x10x1-in. baking pan. Roast 35-45 minutes or until tender, stirring occasionally.

✳ **TEST KITCHEN TIP**
Brussels sprouts are in season between September and May, with peak season between October and February. Select ones that are small and firm and have tightly closed heads with a bright green color. Refrigerate sprouts, unwashed, in an open plastic bag for up to 3 days.

HOW TO ROAST VEGETABLES

- Cut the vegetables into fairly large pieces, cubes or thick slices. Toss the vegetables with a little olive oil (or butter, if the recipe calls for it).

- Spread the veggies in a heavy jelly-roll pan or roasting pan. Line the pan with foil and coat with nonstick cooking spray for easier cleanup. Heavier pans are designed to withstand high heat and will help keep the vegetables from drying out or burning.

- About halfway through cooking time (or at about 25-30 minutes), turn the vegetables over with a spatula, then continue to cook them until they're tender and browned on the edges—about 20 minutes longer.

- Don't be afraid of the high heat—let the veggies sizzle! The heat blisters the vegetables' surfaces, and this is just what you're after.

- Tomatoes, zucchini, summer squash, green beans and eggplant won't take as long to roast as other veggies. Vegetables such as onions, cauliflower, peppers, broccoli, turnips, potatoes, sweet potatoes, carrots, parsnips and beets take much longer to roast, so keep that in mind when planning your meal.

EASY PEASY!

MUSHROOM & PEAS RICE PILAF

Anything goes in rice pilaf, so I add peas and baby portobello mushrooms for color, texture and a touch of comfort.
—Stacy Mullens, Gresham, OR

Start to Finish: 25 min. **Makes:** 6 servings

1 package (6.6 ounces) rice pilaf mix with toasted almonds
1 tablespoon butter
1½ cups fresh or frozen peas
1 cup sliced baby portobello mushrooms

1. Prepare the pilaf mix according to package directions.

2. In a large skillet, heat the butter over medium heat. Add the peas and mushrooms; cook and stir 6-8 minutes or until tender. Stir in rice.

✳

TEST KITCHEN TIP
As long as you're whipping up this Mushroom & Peas Rice Pilaf, why not double or triple the recipe for busy nights? Divide the extra pilaf into 1-cup portions, and transfer each to a resealable freezer storage bag. Squeeze out the air, flatten the bag and seal. Simply take out portions as needed and reheat in the microwave.

HOW TO COOK PEAS, FOUR SIMPLE WAYS

One important note: There's no need to defrost frozen peas before cooking. In these recipes, fresh or frozen peas may be used.

Microwave: Peas, fresh or frozen, can be zapped in a snap. In a microwave-safe dish, combine peas with a tablespoon of water. Cover with a lid or a paper napkin and cook on high for 3-4 minutes. Give the peas a stir and continue to cook for 3-5 minutes more. Taste one (careful, it'll be hot!). If it's tender and hot throughout, it's ready. Drain and serve. (Drain peas in a mesh strainer rather than a colander so they don't get caught or fall through the colander's larger holes.)

Boil: In a saucepan, combine 16 oz. of peas with about ½ cup of water. Bring the liquid to a boil with the lid off. Reduce the heat, cover and let the peas simmer for 3-5 minutes or until tender. Drain off any excess liquid and serve.

Steam: (shown far left, bottom) Pour about an inch of water into a saucepan. Place the peas into a steamer basket and drop the basket into the pan. Bring the water to a boil, then cover the pot. The rising steam will cook the peas. We recommend steaming for 2-4 minutes, testing occasionally along the way. As soon as the peas are tender, they're ready. This is our favorite way to cook fresh peas, which are typically available for a brief time in late spring and early summer and deserve the gentle treatment to preserve their flavor.

Saute: (shown bottom left) This is our favorite method for frozen peas, because it's easy to toss in other ingredients, as in this Mushroom & Peas Rice Pilaf recipe. Begin by heating a tablespoon of butter or oil over medium-high heat. For more flavor, add a chopped onion, sliced fresh mushrooms or minced garlic. Let things cook for a couple of minutes until garlic, mushrooms and/or onions are wilted and soft. Add about 2 cups of peas. Stir them around, still over medium-high heat, until they're heated through and tender, about 3-5 minutes. Add salt and pepper to taste, and consider sprinkling on a bit of your favorite spice or fresh herbs.

OVEN ENTREES

Think you could never make a casserole or meat loaf as good as Mom's? Think again! We'll show you how. And while we're at it, say goodbye to delivery and become a pizza-making pro. Fire up the oven—let's get cookin'!

WEEKNIGHT LASAGNA

My husband and I love lasagna, but it's time-consuming to build and we always end up with too much. Using frozen ravioli solves everything.
—Pamela Nicholson, Festus, MO

Prep: 15 min. **Bake:** 45 min. **Makes:** 6 servings

1 jar (24 ounces) pasta sauce
1 package (25 ounces) frozen meat or cheese ravioli
3 cups fresh baby spinach
1½ cups shredded part-skim mozzarella cheese

1. Preheat oven to 350°. In a small saucepan, heat sauce 5-7 minutes over medium heat or just until simmering, stirring occasionally.

2. Spread ½ cup sauce into a greased 11x7-in. baking dish. Layer with half of the ravioli, 1½ cups spinach, ½ cup cheese and half of the remaining sauce. Repeat layers, then sprinkle with the remaining cheese.

3. Bake, uncovered, 45-50 minutes or until edges are bubbly and cheese is melted. Let stand 5 minutes before serving.

✳

Want to save a bit of cash? Buy cheese in bulk and shred it yourself. Keep in mind that 4 ounces of cheese equals 1 cup shredded. Once shredded, store cheese in an airtight container in the refrigerator.

HAM & VEGGIE CASSEROLE

I've paired ham with broccoli and cauliflower for years. To complete this casserole dinner, I pass around the dinner rolls.
—Sherri Melotik, Oak Creek, WI

Start to Finish: 30 min. **Makes:** 4 servings

1 package (16 ounces) frozen
   broccoli florets
1 package (16 ounces) frozen
   cauliflower
2 teaspoons plus 2 tablespoons
   butter, divided
¼ cup seasoned bread crumbs
2 tablespoons all-purpose flour
1½ cups 2% milk
¾ cup shredded sharp cheddar
   cheese
½ cup grated Parmesan cheese
1½ cups cubed fully cooked ham
   (about 8 ounces)
¼ teaspoon pepper

1. Preheat oven to 425°. Cook broccoli and cauliflower according to package directions; drain.

2. Meanwhile, in a small skillet, melt 2 teaspoons butter. Add the bread crumbs; cook and stir over medium heat 2-3 minutes or until lightly toasted. Remove from heat.

3. In a large saucepan, melt remaining butter over medium heat. Stir in flour until smooth; gradually whisk in milk. Bring to a boil, stirring constantly; cook and stir 1-2 minutes or until thickened. Remove from heat; stir in cheeses until blended. Stir in ham, pepper and vegetables.

4. Transfer to a greased 8-in. square baking dish. Sprinkle with toasted crumbs. Bake, uncovered, until heated through, 10-15 minutes.

HOW TO MAKE HOMEMADE BREAD CRUMBS

- Pulse three to four bread slices in a food processor until coarse crumbs form. If desired, you can sprinkle in some dried herbs to add flavor.

- Spread crumbs on an ungreased baking sheet and bake at 350° for 8-10 minutes or until dried and just starting to brown, stirring after 5 minutes.

PAN-ROASTED CHICKEN & VEGETABLES

This one-dish meal tastes like it needs hours of hands-on time to put together, but it takes just minutes to prep the simple ingredients. So easy!
—Sherri Melotik, Oak Creek, WI

Prep: 15 min. **Bake:** 45 min. **Makes:** 6 servings

2 pounds red potatoes (about 6 medium), cut into ¾-inch pieces
1 large onion, coarsely chopped
2 tablespoons olive oil
3 garlic cloves, minced
1¼ teaspoons salt, divided
1 teaspoon dried rosemary, crushed, divided
¾ teaspoon pepper, divided
½ teaspoon paprika
6 bone-in chicken thighs (about 2¼ pounds), skin removed
6 cups fresh baby spinach (about 6 ounces)

1. Preheat oven to 425°. In a large bowl, combine potatoes, onion, oil, garlic, ¾ teaspoon salt, ½ teaspoon rosemary and ½ teaspoon pepper; toss to coat. Transfer to a 15x10x1-in. baking pan coated with cooking spray.

2. In a small bowl, mix paprika and the remaining salt, rosemary and pepper. Sprinkle chicken with paprika mixture; arrange over vegetables. Roast until a thermometer inserted in chicken reads 170°-175° and vegetables are just tender, 35-40 minutes.

3. Remove chicken to a serving platter; keep warm. Top vegetables with baby spinach. Roast until the vegetables are tender and the spinach is wilted, 8-10 minutes longer. Stir vegetables to combine; serve with chicken.

✳

TEST KITCHEN TIP
Make sure chicken is fully cooked by inserting a thermometer into the thickest part of the thigh (without touching the bone). Chicken thighs are safe to eat at 165°, but we prefer the taste and texture when they're cooked to 170-175°F.

ONE PAN
WONDER!

MY MOM'S BEST MEAT LOAF

The Rice Krispies used in this recipe are my mom's secret ingredient. While they may seem odd, they help hold the meat loaf together. And once they're cooked, no one realizes they're even there.
—Kelly Simmons, Hopkinsville, KY

Prep: 10 min. **Bake:** 1 hour + standing **Makes:** 8 servings

½ cup chili sauce
¼ cup ketchup
2 cups Rice Krispies
1 medium onion, finely chopped
1 small green or sweet red pepper, finely chopped
¾ cup shredded part-skim mozzarella cheese
1 large egg, lightly beaten
½ teaspoon salt
¼ teaspoon pepper
2 pounds ground beef

1. Preheat oven to 350°. In a small bowl, mix chili sauce and ketchup. In a large bowl, combine Rice Krispies, onion, green pepper, cheese, egg, salt and pepper; stir in half of the chili sauce mixture. Add ground beef; mix lightly but thoroughly.

2. Transfer the beef mixture to an ungreased 9x5-in. loaf pan. Make a shallow indentation down center of loaf. Spread remaining chili sauce mixture over loaf, being sure to fill indentation.

3. Bake 60-70 minutes or until a thermometer reads 160°; use a turkey baster to remove the drippings every 20 minutes. Let stand 10 minutes before slicing.

Note: This recipe was tested with Heinz chili sauce.

WHY YOU'LL LOVE IT...

"My new favorite recipe! I have been looking for a meat loaf that is tasty, classic, easy to prepare and fit for a picky eater (describing myself here!). This recipe is perfect, and the sauce completes it!"
—JENNA092, TASTEOFHOME.COM

ULTIMATE POT ROAST

When juicy pot roast simmers in garlic, onions and veggies, everyone comes running to ask, "When can we eat?" The answer? Just wait—it will be worth it.
—Nick Iverson, Milwaukee, WI

Prep: 55 min. **Bake:** 2 hours **Makes:** 8 servings

- 1 boneless beef chuck-eye or other chuck roast (3 to 4 pounds)
- 2 teaspoons pepper
- 2 teaspoons salt, divided
- 2 tablespoons canola oil
- 2 medium onions, cut into 1-inch pieces
- 2 celery ribs, chopped
- 3 garlic cloves, minced
- 1 tablespoon tomato paste
- 1 tablespoon minced fresh thyme or 1 teaspoon dried thyme
- 2 bay leaves
- 1 cup dry red wine or reduced-sodium beef broth
- 2 cups reduced-sodium beef broth
- 1 pound small red potatoes, quartered
- 4 medium parsnips, peeled and cut into 2-inch pieces
- 6 medium carrots, cut into 2-inch pieces
- 1 tablespoon red wine vinegar
- 2 tablespoons minced fresh parsley
  Salt and pepper to taste

1. Preheat oven to 325°. Pat roast dry with a paper towel; tie at 2-in. intervals with kitchen string. Sprinkle roast with pepper and 1½ teaspoons salt. In a Dutch oven, heat oil over medium-high heat. Brown roast on all sides. Remove from pan.

2. Add onions, celery and ½ teaspoon salt to the same pan; cook and stir over medium heat 8-10 minutes or until onions are browned. Add garlic, tomato paste, thyme and bay leaves; cook and stir 1 minute longer.

3. Add wine, stirring to loosen browned bits from pan; stir in broth. Return roast to pan. Arrange potatoes, parsnips and carrots around roast; bring to a boil. Bake, covered, until meat is fork-tender, 2-2½ hours.

4. Remove roast and vegetables from pan; keep warm. Discard bay leaves; skim fat from cooking juices. On stovetop, bring juices to a boil; cook until the liquid is reduced by half (about 1½ cups), 10-12 minutes. Stir in vinegar and parsley; season with salt and pepper to taste.

5. Remove string from roast. Serve with vegetables and sauce.

* Find the perfect dessert to round out this comforting meal. Turn to page 160 to see all sorts of sweet treats.

HOW TO TIE A POT ROAST

(Pictured above, left to right)

- Pat roast dry. Slip a long piece of kitchen string under roast and tie across the grain.

- Continue tying at 2-in. intervals.

- Cut strings and continue with the recipe.

SALSA VERDE CHICKEN CASSEROLE

This is a rich and surprisingly tasty rendition of many Tex-Mex dishes blended into one packed, beautiful casserole. Best of all, it's ready in no time!
—Janet McCormick, Proctorville, OH

Start to Finish: 30 min. **Makes:** 6 servings

2 cups shredded rotisserie chicken
1 cup (8 ounces) sour cream
1½ cups salsa verde, divided
8 corn or flour tortillas (6 inches)
2 cups chopped tomatoes
¼ cup minced fresh cilantro
2 cups shredded Monterey
   Jack cheese
   Optional toppings: avocado slices,
     thinly sliced green onions and
     fresh cilantro leaves

1. Combine the chicken, sour cream and ¾ cup salsa in a small bowl. Spread ¼ cup salsa on the bottom of a greased 8-in. square baking dish.

2. Layer with half each of the tortillas and chicken mixture; sprinkle with the tomatoes, minced cilantro and half of the cheese. Repeat layers with the remaining tortillas, chicken mixture and shredded cheese.

3. Bake casserole, uncovered, at 400° for 20-25 minutes or until bubbly. Serve with remaining salsa and, if desired, optional toppings.

✳

TEST KITCHEN TIPS
Some like it hot! Add sliced jalapenos (fresh or pickled) if you want to kick the flavor up a notch.

When substituting canned tomatoes for fresh, drain them first so you don't end up with soup.

PARMESAN-BREADED PORK CHOPS

Shredded Parmesan and seasoned bread crumbs push the flavor of these juicy chops over the top. The whole family loves this dish that cooks hands-free while I prepare the rest of the meal.
—Hayden Hosick, Corona, CA

Start to Finish: 25 min. **Makes:** 4 servings

4 boneless pork loin chops
  (6 ounces each)
½ teaspoon salt
¼ teaspoon pepper
½ cup garlic and herb bread crumbs
⅓ cup shredded Parmesan cheese
2 large eggs, lightly beaten
2 tablespoons olive oil

1. Preheat oven to 350°. Sprinkle pork chops with salt and pepper. In a shallow bowl, mix bread crumbs and cheese. Place eggs in a separate shallow bowl. Dip pork chops in eggs, then in crumb mixture, patting to help coating adhere.

2. In a 10-in. ovenproof skillet, heat oil over medium heat. Brown pork chops on both sides. Bake 12-15 minutes or until a thermometer reads 145°. Let stand 5 minutes.

WHY YOU'LL LOVE IT...

"Super simple and so delicious! Great company dish, since you can prep it up to the baking part and have everything cleaned up ahead of time. Everyone loved these!"

—AMEHART, TASTEOFHOME.COM

THERE'S BEER IN THE CRUST!

SPINACH & ARTICHOKE PIZZA

My from-scratch pizza has a whole wheat crust flavored with beer.
Top it with spinach, artichoke hearts, tomatoes and fresh basil.
—Raymonde Bourgeois, Swastika, ON

Prep: 25 min. **Bake:** 20 min. **Makes:** 6 slices

1½ to 1¾ cups white whole wheat
    flour
1½ teaspoons baking powder
¼ teaspoon salt
¼ teaspoon each dried basil, oregano
    and parsley flakes
¾ cup beer or nonalcoholic beer

TOPPINGS

1½ teaspoons olive oil
1 garlic clove, minced
2 cups shredded Italian cheese
    blend
2 cups fresh baby spinach
1 can (14 ounces) water-packed
    quartered artichoke hearts,
    drained and coarsely chopped
2 medium tomatoes, seeded and
    coarsely chopped
2 tablespoons thinly sliced fresh
    basil

1. Preheat oven to 425°. In a large bowl, whisk 1½ cups flour, baking powder, salt and dried herbs until blended. Add beer, stirring just until moistened.

2. Turn dough onto a well-floured surface; knead gently 6-8 times, adding more flour if needed. Press dough to fit a greased 12-in. pizza pan. Pinch edge to form a rim. Bake 8 minutes or until edge is lightly browned.

3. Mix oil and garlic; spread over crust. Sprinkle with ½ cup cheese; layer with spinach, artichoke hearts and tomatoes. Sprinkle with remaining cheese. Bake 8-10 minutes or until the crust is golden and cheese is melted. Sprinkle with fresh basil.

HOW TO SEED A TOMATO

Seeding a tomato eliminates some of the juice that can make a dish too watery. To seed a tomato, cut the fruit in half horizontally and remove the stem. Holding one half over a bowl, scrape out the seeds with a small spoon or squeeze the tomato to force them out. Then cut as directed in the recipe.

SKILLET & STOVETOP ENTREES

When you need a meal in a flash, look no further than your stovetop. Heat it up for a variety of sizzling main dishes that are sure to satisfy. It's the mighty skillet to the dinnertime rescue!

ONE-POT CHICKEN PESTO PASTA

When the basil in my garden goes nuts, I make pesto and keep it frozen in small containers for the right opportunity, like this saucy one-pot chicken with pasta.
—Kimberly Fenwick, Hobart, IN

Start to Finish: 30 min. **Makes:** 4 servings

1 pound boneless skinless chicken thighs, cut into 1-inch pieces
1 teaspoon salt-free seasoning blend
2 teaspoons olive oil
1 can (14½ ounces) reduced-sodium chicken broth
2 tablespoons lemon juice
1 cup uncooked gemelli or spiral pasta
2 cups fresh broccoli florets
1 cup frozen peas
⅓ cup prepared pesto

1. Toss chicken with seasoning blend. In a large nonstick skillet, heat oil over medium-high heat. Add chicken and brown evenly; remove from pan.

2. In the same pan, combine broth and lemon juice; bring to a boil, stirring to loosen browned bits from pan. Stir in pasta; return to a boil. Reduce heat; simmer, covered, 10 minutes.

3. Add broccoli; cook, covered, 5 minutes. Return chicken to pan; cook, covered, 2-3 minutes longer or until pasta is tender and chicken is no longer pink, stirring occasionally. Add peas; heat through. Stir in pesto.

HOW TO MAKE PESTO
(Pictured bottom right, left to right)

For a fresh twist, prepare your own homemade pesto. You'll be pleasantly surprised by how easy it is to make in a food processor.

You'll need:
2 cups loosely packed basil leaves
1 cup loosely packed Italian parsley
¼ cup slivered almonds, toasted
2 garlic cloves
4 teaspoons grated lemon peel
⅓ cup lemon juice
2 tablespoons honey
½ teaspoon salt
½ cup olive oil
½ cup grated Parmesan cheese

- Place basil, parsley, slivered almonds and garlic in a small food processor; pulse until chopped.

- Add lemon peel, lemon juice, honey and salt; process until blended. Continue processing while gradually adding oil in a steady stream.

- Add cheese; pulse until the mixture is blended.

- Store in an airtight container in the refrigerator for up to a week.

HOW TO MAKE ZUCCHINI NOODLES

(Pictured right)

You'll need:
2 large zucchini (about
   1½ pounds)
2 garlic cloves, minced
1 teaspoon olive oil
¼ teaspoon salt
Spiralizer, vegetable peeler
   or box grater

- Begin by trimming off the ends of zucchini. Depending on your preference, you can keep the skin on or peel it off before turning the vegetable into noodles. Align zucchini so one end meets the blade, then poke the claw insert into the opposite end so it's held in place. Crank the spiralizer handle, applying light pressure to feed the zucchini into the grating blades. Keep turning until the zucchini has been completely spiralized...and that's it! The strands you've created are zucchini noodles.

- Add oil to a large nonstick skillet over medium-high heat. Toss in the zucchini noodles (with minced garlic if you want more flavor). Cook for 1-2 minutes. Make sure the zucchini cooks only slightly, to preserve its fresh, crunchy texture. As the zoodles cook, toss them constantly with a pair of tongs so they don't overcook. When finished, sprinkle with salt.

30 MINUTES 'TIL DINNER

BLACKENED TILAPIA WITH ZUCCHINI NOODLES

I love quick and bright meals like this one-skillet wonder. It replaces pasta with good-for-you zoodles for one awesome meal!
—Tammy Brownlow, Dallas, TX

Start to Finish: 30 min. **Makes:** 4 servings

 2 large zucchini (about 1½ pounds)
1½ teaspoons ground cumin
 ¾ teaspoon salt, divided
 ½ teaspoon smoked paprika
 ½ teaspoon pepper
 ¼ teaspoon garlic powder
 4 tilapia fillets (6 ounces each)
 2 teaspoons olive oil
 2 garlic cloves, minced
 1 cup pico de gallo

1. Trim ends of zucchini. Using a spiralizer, cut zucchini into thin strands.

2. Mix cumin, ½ teaspoon salt, smoked paprika, pepper and garlic powder; sprinkle generously onto both sides of tilapia. In a large nonstick skillet, heat oil over medium-high heat. In batches, cook tilapia until fish just begins to flake easily with a fork, 2-3 minutes per side. Remove from pan; keep warm.

3. In the same pan, cook zucchini with garlic over medium-high heat until slightly softened, 1-2 minutes, tossing noodles constantly with tongs (do not overcook). Sprinkle with remaining salt. Serve with tilapia and pico de gallo.

Note: If a spiralizer is not available, zucchini may also be cut into ribbons using a vegetable peeler. Saute as directed, increasing time as necessary.

✳
TEST KITCHEN TIP
Overcooking fish dries it out, so it's important to know how to tell when it's done. For fillets, check by inserting a fork at an angle into the thickest portion of the fish and gently parting the flesh. When it's opaque (in other words, not see-through) and flakes into sections, it is cooked completely. A translucent appearance means it needs to cook a little longer.

MAPLE-DIJON CHICKEN

Eating dinner as a family every night is really important to us, and this recipe is one that we all love. It's our favorite skillet chicken dish.
—Courtney Stultz, Weir, KS

Start to Finish: 30 min. **Makes:** 4 servings

1 pound boneless skinless chicken breasts, cut into 1-inch-thick strips
½ teaspoon dried rosemary, crushed
½ teaspoon dried thyme
½ teaspoon pepper
¼ teaspoon salt
1 tablespoon coconut oil or olive oil
½ cup chopped onion
1 garlic clove, minced
⅓ cup Dijon mustard
3 tablespoons maple syrup

Toss chicken with seasonings. In a large skillet, heat oil over medium heat; saute chicken 10 minutes. Add onion and garlic; cook and stir 5 minutes. Stir in mustard and syrup; cook and stir until sauce is caramelized and chicken is no longer pink, 5-7 minutes.

COMMON STOVETOP COOKING TECHNIQUES

Saute: Add a small amount of oil to a hot skillet and heat over medium-high heat. For best results, cut the food into uniformly sized pieces before adding. Don't overcrowd the pan. Stir frequently while cooking.

Sear: Heat oil in a large skillet over medium-high heat until it almost begins to smoke. Pat food dry. Cook the food until a deeply colored crust has formed. Be careful not to crowd the pan, and reduce heat if food browns too quickly.

Braise: Season meat; coat with flour if recipe directs. In a Dutch oven, brown meat in oil in batches. To ensure nice browning, do not crowd. Set meat aside; cook vegetables, adding flour if recipe directs. Add broth gradually, stirring to deglaze the pan and keep lumps from forming. Return meat to pan and stir until mixture comes to a boil.

Steam: Place a steamer basket or bamboo steamer in a pan with water. Bring to a boil (boiling water should not touch the steamer) and place food in basket; cover and steam. Add more boiling water to pan as necessary, making sure the pan doesn't run dry and water doesn't touch the steamer.

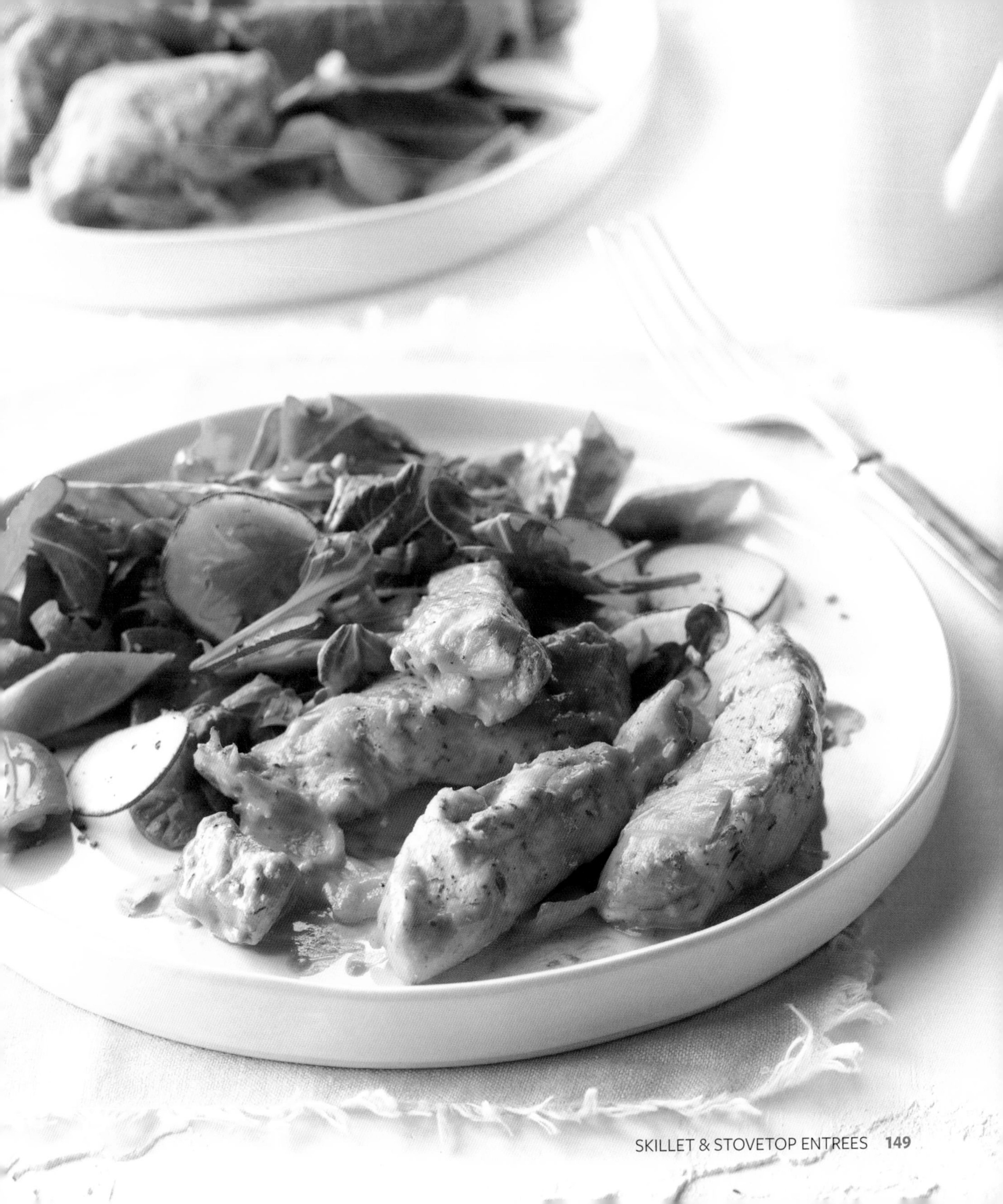

BEST SPAGHETTI & MEATBALLS

One evening, we had unexpected company. I had some of these meatballs in the freezer, so I warmed them up as appetizers. Everyone raved! This classic recipe makes a big batch and is perfect for entertaining.
—Mary Lou Koskella, Prescott, AZ

Prep: 30 min. **Cook:** 2 hours **Makes:** 16 servings

2 tablespoons olive oil
1½ cups chopped onions
3 garlic cloves, minced
2 cans (12 ounces each) tomato paste
3 cups water
1 can (29 ounces) tomato sauce
⅓ cup minced fresh parsley
1 tablespoon dried basil
2 teaspoons salt
½ teaspoon pepper

MEATBALLS
4 large eggs, lightly beaten
2 cups soft bread cubes (cut into ¼-inch pieces)
1½ cups whole milk
1 cup grated Parmesan cheese
3 garlic cloves, minced
2 teaspoons salt
½ teaspoon pepper
3 pounds ground beef
2 tablespoons canola oil
2 pounds spaghetti, cooked

✳ TEST KITCHEN TIP
As an alternative to the skillet, grab a sheet pan. The meatballs may be placed on a baking sheet and roasted in a 375º oven for about 20 minutes.

1. In a Dutch oven, heat olive oil over medium heat. Add onions; saute until softened. Add garlic; cook 1 minute longer. Stir in the tomato paste; cook 3-5 minutes. Add next six ingredients. Bring to a boil. Reduce heat; simmer, covered, for 50 minutes.

2. Combine the first seven meatball ingredients. Add beef; mix lightly but thoroughly. Shape into 1½-in. balls.

3. In a large skillet, heat canola oil over medium heat. Add meatballs; brown in batches until no longer pink. Drain. Add to sauce; bring to a boil. Reduce heat; simmer, covered, until flavors are blended, about 1 hour, stirring occasionally. Serve with hot cooked spaghetti.

HOW TO MAKE SPAGHETTI & MEATBALLS
(Pictured left, clockwise from top left)

- Before adding the remaining sauce ingredients, cook the tomato paste, onions and garlic together a few minutes to caramelize the sugars in the paste, boosting the bright tomato flavor of the sauce.

- Add the rest of the sauce ingredients, then put a lid on it and step away. Simmering helps meld and amplify the flavors of the sauce, so don't skimp on the simmering time.

- The best time to make the meatballs is while the sauce is simmering.

- Wet your hands before rolling the meatballs so the meat doesn't stick to your fingers. Re-wet hands every two or three meatballs.

- Brown the meatballs in batches to avoid crowding the pan. This is key!

- Next, add the meatballs to the sauce. This helps the flavors blend as the meat cooks through.

To freeze: For a convenient freezer option, simmer the meatballs and sauce as directed. Cool, then place in freezer containers. Make sure the meatballs are covered with sauce so they don't dry out. Freeze. To reheat, place meatballs and sauce in a Dutch oven over medium heat or in a slow cooker on low until heated through.

STOVETOP TURKEY TETRAZZINI

A very special aunt shared this fun spin on creamy tetrazzini. We think it's even better as leftovers the next day.
—Tasia Cox, Niceville, FL

Start to Finish: 30 min. **Makes:** 6 servings

8 ounces uncooked spaghetti
2 tablespoons butter
1 cup sliced fresh mushrooms
1 celery rib, chopped
½ cup chopped onion
1 package (8 ounces) cream cheese, cubed
1 can (10½ ounces) condensed chicken broth, undiluted
2 cups chopped cooked turkey
1 jar (2 ounces) diced pimientos, drained
¼ teaspoon salt
¼ cup grated Parmesan cheese

1. Cook spaghetti according to package directions; drain. Meanwhile, in a large skillet, heat butter over medium-high heat. Add the mushrooms, celery and onion; cook and stir 6-8 minutes or until mushrooms are tender.

2. Add cream cheese and broth; cook, uncovered, over low heat 4-6 minutes or until blended, stirring occasionally. Add turkey, pimientos, salt and cooked spaghetti; heat through, tossing to coat. Serve with Parmesan cheese.

✳

TEST KITCHEN TIP
Select mushrooms with firm, smooth caps and closed gills; avoid ones with cracks, brown spots or blemishes. You can store unwashed, loose mushrooms in the refrigerator for 5-10 days. Keep mushrooms away from veggies with strong aromas.

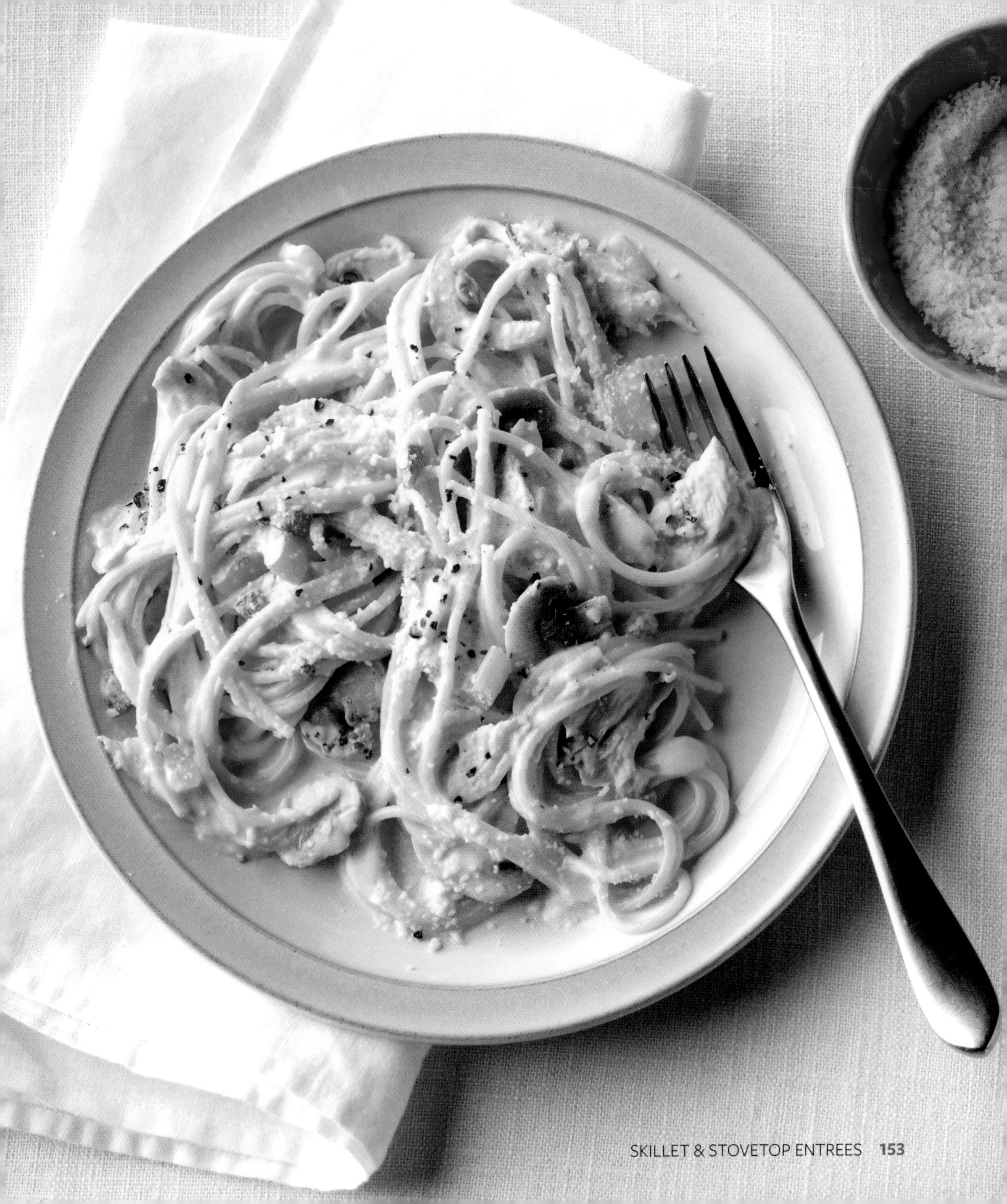

SKILLET NACHOS

My mom gave me a fundraiser cookbook, and the recipe I've used most is for skillet nachos. The whole family is on board. For toppings, think sour cream, tomatoes, jalapeno and red onion.
—Judy Hughes, Waverly, KS

Start to Finish: 30 min. **Makes:** 6 servings

1 pound ground beef
1 can (14½ ounces) diced tomatoes, undrained
1 cup fresh or frozen corn, thawed
¾ cup uncooked instant rice
½ cup water
1 envelope taco seasoning
½ teaspoon salt
1 cup shredded Colby-Monterey Jack cheese
1 package (16 ounces) tortilla chips
Optional toppings: sour cream, sliced fresh jalapenos, shredded lettuce and lime wedges

1. In a large cast-iron or other skillet, cook beef over medium heat for 6-8 minutes or until no longer pink, breaking into crumbles; drain. Stir in tomatoes, corn, rice, water, taco seasoning and salt. Bring to a boil. Reduce heat; simmer, covered, for 8-10 minutes until rice is tender and mixture is slightly thickened.

2. Remove from heat; sprinkle with cheese. Let stand, covered, 5 minutes or until cheese is melted. Divide tortilla chips among six plates; spoon beef mixture over chips. Serve with toppings as desired.

HOW TO SEASON A CAST-IRON SKILLET

Is your food sticking to the cast iron? It's time for a reseasoning!

Seasoning is the process of adhering oil to the pan's surface to create a nonstick coating. New pans are factory-seasoned, but here's how to reseason an older cast-iron pan and give it new life:

- Line the lowest oven rack with foil and preheat the oven to 350°.

- Scrub the pan with hot, soapy water and a stiff brush to remove any rust.

- Towel dry and apply a thin coat of vegetable oil to the entire pan—outside and handle included.

- Place pan on top oven rack, upside down; bake for 1 hour.

- Turn off the oven and leave the pan inside to cool. Now seasoned, it's ready for you to cook with.

- For daily cleaning, rinse with hot water, using a stiff nylon brush to remove residue. Avoid dish soap; it removes seasoning. And don't submerge a hot pan in cold water; it can crack. Towel dry and apply a light coat of oil while the pan is warm.

CHICKEN BURRITO SKILLET

We love Mexican night at our house, and I love to re-create dishes from our favorite restaurants. This burrito-inspired dish is ready for the table in almost no time!
—Krista Marshall, Fort Wayne, IN

Prep: 15 min. **Cook:** 30 min. **Makes:** 6 servings

1 pound boneless skinless chicken breasts, cut into 1½-inch pieces
⅛ teaspoon salt
⅛ teaspoon pepper
2 tablespoons olive oil, divided
1 cup uncooked long grain rice
1 can (15 ounces) black beans, rinsed and drained
1 can (14½ ounces) diced tomatoes, drained
1 teaspoon ground cumin
½ teaspoon onion powder
½ teaspoon garlic powder
½ teaspoon chili powder
2½ cups reduced-sodium chicken broth
1 cup shredded Mexican cheese blend
1 medium tomato, chopped
3 green onions, chopped

1. Toss chicken with salt and pepper. In a large skillet, heat 1 tablespoon oil over medium-high heat; saute chicken until browned, about 2 minutes. Remove from pan.

2. In same pan, heat remaining oil over medium-high heat; saute rice until lightly browned, 1-2 minutes. Stir in beans, canned tomatoes, seasonings and broth; bring to a boil. Place chicken on top (do not stir into rice). Simmer, covered, until rice is tender and chicken is no longer pink, 20-25 minutes.

3. Remove from heat; sprinkle with cheese. Let stand, covered, until the cheese is melted. Top with tomato and green onions.

✳

TEST KITCHEN TIP
Any can of beans you have in your pantry will taste great in this recipe. We particularly like pintos and kidney beans here. Create a healthier dish by using brown rice instead of white.

HOW TO POACH AN EGG

(Pictured above)

- Place 2-3 in. of water in a pan or pot. Turn the heat up and bring the water to a boil. Break cold eggs, one at a time, into small ramekins or cups. Have them ready beside the stove. Turn the boiling water down to a gentle simmer. Bubbles should gently float up from the bottom of the pan. Hold an egg bowl over the water as close as you comfortably can. Nice and easy, slip an egg into the water. Give it a few seconds to gather itself. Repeat.

- Cook, uncovered, 3-5 minutes or until whites are completely set and yolks begin to thicken but are not yet hard. Using a slotted spoon, lift eggs out of water. Drain on paper towels.

- Enjoy immediately!

STIR-FRY RICE BOWL

My meatless version of Korean bibimbap *is tasty, pretty and easy to tweak for different spice-level preferences.*
—Devon Delaney, Westport, Connecticut

Start to Finish: 30 min. **Makes:** 4 servings

1 tablespoon canola oil
2 medium carrots, julienned
1 medium zucchini, julienned
½ cup sliced baby portobello
  mushrooms
1 cup bean sprouts
1 cup fresh baby spinach
1 tablespoon water
1 tablespoon reduced-sodium soy
  sauce
1 tablespoon chili garlic sauce
4 large eggs
3 cups hot cooked brown rice
1 teaspoon sesame oil

1. In a large skillet, heat canola oil over medium-high heat. Add carrots, zucchini and mushrooms; cook and stir 3-5 minutes or until carrots are crisp-tender. Add bean sprouts, baby spinach, water, soy sauce and chili sauce; cook and stir just until spinach is wilted. Remove from heat; keep warm.

2. Place 2-3 in. of water in a large skillet with high sides. Bring to a boil; adjust heat to maintain a gentle simmer. Break cold eggs, one at a time, into small dishes; holding a dish close to surface of water, slip egg into water; repeat.

3. Cook, uncovered, 3-5 minutes or until whites are completely set and yolks begin to thicken but are not hard. Using a slotted spoon, lift eggs out of water.

4. Serve cooked rice in bowls; top with vegetables. Drizzle with sesame oil. Top each serving with a poached egg.

✱
TEST KITCHEN TIP
When a recipe calls for ingredients to be julienned, cut those foods into long thin strips much like matchsticks.

* Turn to page 316 for a breakdown of common cooking terms.

DAZZLING DESSERTS

Hooray! It's time for everyone's favorite part of the meal. (It's safe to assume that, right?) Don't be intimidated by gorgeous cakes, decadent brownies or from-scratch chocolate chip cookies anymore. You've got this!

FROSTED TURTLE BROWNIES

Homemade brownies are a sweet addition to the appetizer table at parties and casual game-day get-togethers. Your guests might forget the score, but I guarantee they'll remember these brownies!
—Sherry Miller, Columbia Heights, MN

Prep: 20 min. **Bake:** 25 min. + chilling **Makes:** 2 dozen

1 cup butter, softened
2 cups sugar
2 teaspoons vanilla extract
4 large eggs
1 cup baking cocoa
1 cup all-purpose flour
½ teaspoon baking powder
¼ teaspoon salt

TOPPING
3 cups confectioners' sugar
¾ cup baking cocoa
½ cup butter, melted
⅓ cup 2% milk
¾ teaspoon vanilla extract
1 cup chopped pecans, toasted
12 caramels
1 tablespoon heavy whipping cream

1. In a large bowl, cream butter and sugar until light and fluffy. Add vanilla. Add eggs, one at a time, beating well after each addition. Combine the cocoa, flour, baking powder and salt; gradually add to butter mixture.

2. Spread into a greased 13x9-in. baking pan. Bake at 350° for 23-28 minutes or until a toothpick inserted in center comes out clean (do not overbake). Cool on a wire rack.

3. In a large bowl, beat confectioners' sugar, cocoa, butter, milk and vanilla until fluffy. Frost brownies. Sprinkle with pecans. Refrigerate for at least 1 hour.

4. In a microwave, melt caramels with cream; stir until smooth. Drizzle over the brownies.

HOW TO SOFTEN BUTTER QUICKLY

Cut the butter stick in half so you have two long rectangles side by side. Stack them together and slice again. This yields four butter strips. Keep them stacked, and then slice perpendicular to your cuts. The butter will fall into cubes, and the cubes will soften fairly quickly, in about 15 minutes. (Now's a good time to measure and prep the remaining ingredients.)

HOW TO GREASE A TUBE PAN

(Pictured right)

You'll need:
Vegetable shortening
Paper towels
Flour
Spoon

- Fold a sheet of paper towel and dip it into the shortening. You'll need plenty, so scoop out a big glob of the stuff. Then, as though washing the pan with a soapy sponge, spread the shortening around, making sure to coat all of its nooks and crannies.

- Take a spoonful of flour and lightly dust the greased pan. If you're worried about the flour clumping, sift it into the pan using a fine-mesh sieve. Next, pick up the pan, gently tapping and rotating it to create a thin, even coating of flour across the pan's interior.

  Test Kitchen tip: For chocolate cakes, dust with cocoa instead of flour to preserve the rich color of the cake.

- Shake out the excess flour. Turn the pan upside down over the sink and gently tap it against the edge of the sink or faucet. (Doing this at the sink makes for much easier cleanup later.)

GLAZED GINGERBREAD CAKE

This is a favorite dessert during the holidays and at special occasions. The glaze on top is simple; since the cake itself is so delicious, I didn't want anything that would cover up its flavor.
—Edith Ekstedt, Paso Robles, CA

Prep: 25 min. **Bake:** 40 min. + cooling **Makes:** 12 servings

CAKE
- 1 cup raisins
- 1 cup molasses
- ½ cup packed brown sugar
- ½ cup canola oil
- ⅓ cup each strong brewed coffee and orange juice
- 2 tablespoons water
- 3 large eggs
- 3 cups all-purpose flour
- ¼ cup nonfat dry milk powder
- 1 tablespoon ground ginger
- 1 tablespoon orange zest
- 1 teaspoon cream of tartar
- 1 teaspoon baking soda
- ½ teaspoon each ground cinnamon, mace and nutmeg

GLAZE
- 2½ cups confectioners' sugar
- ¼ cup 2% milk
- 2 tablespoons butter, melted
- ¼ teaspoon vanilla extract

1. Preheat oven to 350°. Grease and flour a 10-in. fluted tube pan. Place raisins in a small bowl; add boiling water to cover and let stand 5 minutes. Drain.

2. In a large bowl, whisk molasses, brown sugar, oil, coffee, orange juice and water until blended. In a small bowl, beat eggs on high speed 3-4 minutes or until thick and lemon-colored. In another bowl, whisk remaining cake ingredients. Add to molasses mixture alternately with eggs, mixing just until combined. Fold in raisins.

3. Transfer to prepared pan. Bake 40-45 minutes or until a toothpick inserted in the center comes out with moist crumbs (do not overbake). Cool 10 minutes before removing from pan to a wire rack to cool completely.

4. In a small bowl, mix glaze ingredients until smooth. Pour over cake.

Note: For easier removal of cakes, use solid shortening to grease plain and fluted tube pans.

SECRETS FOR SUCCESSFUL CAKE

- Cool cakes for 10 minutes in the pan unless the recipe states otherwise. Loosen the cake by running a knife around the edge of the pan. Turn the cake onto a wire rack, place another rack over the cake and flip right side up. Cool completely before filling or frosting unless the recipe says to do otherwise.

- Pour thinner batters into pans, then tap pans on the counter to remove air bubbles. Spoon firmer batters into pans, then spread gently with a spoon to even out.

- Fill pans half to three-fourths full of cake batter. Thinner batters rise more than heavy batters, so for thin batters, only fill pans to half full.

EASY FRESH STRAWBERRY PIE

When it comes to making pie, it doesn't get much easier (or prettier) than this lovely recipe.
—Sue Jurack, Mequon, WI

Prep: 20 min. + cooling **Bake:** 15 min. + chilling **Makes:** 6-8 servings

1 unbaked pastry shell (9 inches)
¾ cup sugar
2 tablespoons cornstarch
1 cup water
1 package (3 ounces) strawberry gelatin
4 cups sliced fresh strawberries
Fresh mint, optional

* See page 27 for how to make homemade whipped cream to top the pie.

1. Line unpricked pastry shell with a double thickness of heavy-duty foil. Bake at 450° for 8 minutes. Remove foil; bake 5 minutes longer. Cool on a wire rack.

2. In a small saucepan, combine the sugar, cornstarch and water until smooth. Bring to a boil; cook and stir for 2 minutes or until thickened. Remove from the heat; stir in gelatin until dissolved. Refrigerate for 15-20 minutes or until slightly cooled.

3. Meanwhile, arrange strawberries in the crust. Pour gelatin mixture over berries. Refrigerate until set. Garnish with mint if desired.

PIE POINTERS

- When making pie crust from scratch, choose dull-finish aluminum or glass pie plates for the best, crispest crusts. Shiny pans can produce soggy crusts.

- Because of the high fat content in pie pastry, do not grease the pie plate unless the recipe calls for it.

- When rolling out a homemade pie pastry, you'll need a floured surface. However, keep in mind that the less flour you use while rolling, the flakier and lighter the pie pastry will be.

- If a recipe calls for prebaking a pie crust with pie weights, such as dried uncooked beans or rice, don't skip this step! The weights prevent the bottom of the crust from puffing up and the sides from shrinking and slipping down during baking. Important note: Do not eat the beans or rice after.

✳

TEST KITCHEN TIP
You can use whole fresh strawberries and arrange them pointed side up in the pastry shell for a different presentation. This variation is also a time-saver, because the berries only need hulling (not slicing).

EASY AS
PIE!

CHEWY SALTED PEANUT BARS

My family has been making this recipe for generations. Whenever we get together, someone offers to bring the crunchy bars.
—Ann Marie Heinz, Sturgeon Bay, WI

Prep: 10 min. **Bake:** 20 min. + cooling **Makes:** 2 dozen

1½ cups all-purpose flour
¾ cup packed brown sugar
½ cup cold butter, cubed
2 cups lightly salted dry roasted peanuts
1 cup butterscotch chips
½ cup light corn syrup
2 tablespoons butter

1. Preheat oven to 350°. Line a 13x9-in. baking pan with foil, letting ends extend up sides; grease foil. In a small bowl, mix flour and brown sugar; cut in butter until crumbly. Press into prepared pan. Bake 8-10 minutes or until lightly browned. Sprinkle peanuts over crust.

2. In a small saucepan, melt the butterscotch chips, corn syrup and butter over medium heat; stir until smooth. Drizzle over the peanuts. Bake 6-8 minutes longer or until bubbly. Cool completely in the pan on a wire rack. Lifting with foil, remove from pan. Cut into bars.

✳

TEST KITCHEN TIP
To cut these bars easily, use a serrated knife and cut downward (not in a sawing motion).

WHY YOU'LL LOVE IT...

"These bars were easy enough that the kids could help! We used honey-roasted peanuts because that's what I had on hand. I also added about ½ cup of semisweet chocolate chips because, well, chocolate."

—JSTOWELLSUPERMOM, TASTEOFHOME.COM

CHOCOLATE CAKE WITH CHOCOLATE FROSTING

I once sent this rich chocolate cake to my kids' teachers. It vanished, so I had to make another one!
—Megan Moelbert, Springville, NY

Prep: 40 min. **Bake:** 30 min. + cooling **Makes:** 16 servings

2 cups sugar
2 cups water
⅔ cup canola oil
2 tablespoons white vinegar
2 teaspoons vanilla extract
3 cups all-purpose flour
⅓ cup plus 1 tablespoon baking cocoa, sifted
2 teaspoons baking soda
1 teaspoon salt

FROSTING
3¾ cups confectioners' sugar
⅓ cup baking cocoa
1 cup butter, softened
1 teaspoon vanilla extract
3 to 5 tablespoons 2% milk

1. Preheat oven to 350°. Line bottoms of two greased 9-in. round baking pans with parchment paper; grease paper.

2. In a large bowl, beat sugar, water, oil, vinegar and vanilla until well blended. In a large bowl, whisk flour, sifted cocoa, baking soda and salt; gradually add to sugar mixture, beating until smooth.

3. Transfer batter to prepared pans. Bake 30-35 minutes or until a toothpick inserted in the center comes out clean. Cool in pans for 10 minutes before removing to wire racks; remove paper. Cool completely.

4. For frosting, sift confectioners' sugar and cocoa together. In a large bowl, beat butter and vanilla until blended. Beat in confectioners' sugar mixture alternately with enough milk to reach desired consistency. Spread frosting between layers and over top and sides of cake.

For chocolate sheet cake: Make batter as directed and transfer to a greased 13x9-in. baking pan. Bake in a preheated 350° oven for 30-35 minutes or until a toothpick inserted in center comes out clean. Frosting recipe may be halved.

FANCY FROSTING TIPS

- Always sift confectioners' sugar before using it for frosting (or use a whisk to break up lumps if you don't have a sifter). If there are any lumps in the sugar, there will be lumps in the frosting.

- Frosting needs to be the right consistency for spreading and decorating. If it's too thin, add a little confectioners' sugar. If it's too thick, add a little milk.

HOW TO DECORATE CAKES WITH A SPOON-SWIRL TECHNIQUE

(Pictured left)

- Scoop a generous amount of frosting onto the back of the spoon.

- Place the spoon on the cake with its tip in the 12 o'clock position, then swirl the spoon in a half circle to the left, ending in the 6 o'clock position. Repeat until cake is covered.

HOW TO MAKE SPRITZ COOKIES

(Pictured above, left to right)

- Creaming butter and sugar until fluffy incorporates air into the batter, giving cookies a lighter texture. Butter and cream cheese blend best when they're softened but not warm.

- Beating in the flour gradually (instead of adding it all at once) allows the flour to be thoroughly mixed in. More importantly, it cuts down on mess and actually saves time.

- Fit a cookie press with the disk of your choice. Rolling the dough into a cylinder shape makes it easier to insert into the press. The dough should be cool, but not too stiff.

- When making pressed cookies, use ungreased baking sheets so the raw dough will stick. Hold the press against the pan—not above it—when releasing the dough. Never press spritz dough onto a warm cookie sheet.

SPRITZ SANDWICH COOKIES

*I smear my buttery spritz cookies with Biscoff spread, which is
a nut butter alternative that's made from ground Biscoff cookies.*
—Linda Sweet, Cornwall, NY

Prep: 40 min. **Bake:** 10 min./batch **Makes:** 5½ dozen

1½ cups butter, softened
1 cup sugar
1 large egg
2 tablespoons 2% milk
2 teaspoons vanilla extract
3½ cups all-purpose flour
1 teaspoon baking powder
1 teaspoon ground cinnamon
Colored sprinkles
⅔ cup Biscoff spread

1. Preheat oven to 375°. In a large bowl, cream butter and sugar until light and fluffy. Beat in egg, milk and vanilla. In another bowl, whisk flour, baking powder and cinnamon; gradually beat into creamed mixture.

2. Using a cookie press fitted with a disk, press dough 1 in. apart onto ungreased baking sheets. Sprinkle with sprinkles. Bake 6-8 minutes or until set (do not brown). Remove from pans to wire racks to cool completely.

3. Spread about 1 teaspoon Biscoff on the bottoms of half of the cookies; top with remaining cookies.

To freeze: Transfer dough to a resealable plastic freezer bag; freeze. To use, thaw dough in refrigerator overnight or until soft enough to press. Prepare and bake cookies as directed.

COOKIE TROUBLESHOOTING

- Separate soft and crisp cookies in separate airtight containers. If you mix them, the moisture from the softer cookies will affect the texture of the crisp cookies.

- Be patient! Give cookies time to fully cool before either packing them up or frosting them.

- To keep cookies from being too tough, be careful not to overmix them. In general, the instructions will provide a clear idea of how much to mix.

✳
TEST KITCHEN TIP
Look for Biscoff creamy cookie spread near the peanut butter in the grocery store.

TRIPLE BERRY NO-BAKE CHEESECAKE

I've made many cheesecakes and enjoy them all, but they're usually time-consuming. When I first tried this recipe, my husband said it was better than the baked ones, and that was a big plus for me!
—Joyce Mummau, Sugarcreek, OH

Prep: 20 min. + chilling **Makes:** 12 servings (3⅓ cups topping)

- 1½ cups graham cracker crumbs
- ⅓ cup packed brown sugar
- ½ teaspoon ground cinnamon
- ⅓ cup butter, melted

FILLING
- 2 packages (8 ounces each) cream cheese, softened
- ⅓ cup sugar
- 2 teaspoons lemon juice
- 2 cups heavy whipping cream

TOPPING
- 2 cups sliced fresh strawberries
- 1 cup fresh blueberries
- 1 cup fresh raspberries
- 2 tablespoons sugar

1. In a small bowl, mix cracker crumbs, brown sugar and cinnamon; stir in butter. Press onto bottom and 1 in. up sides of an ungreased 9-in. springform pan. Refrigerate 30 minutes.

2. In a large bowl, beat cream cheese, sugar and lemon juice until smooth. Gradually add cream; beat until stiff peaks form. Transfer to prepared crust. Refrigerate, covered, overnight.

3. In a bowl, gently toss berries with sugar. Let stand 15-30 minutes or until juices are released from berries.

4. With a knife, loosen sides of cheesecake from pan; remove rim. Serve cheesecake with topping.

HOW TO MAKE THE PERFECT CHEESECAKE

- To avoid lumps, begin with softened cream cheese. Forgot to soften the cream cheese? Remove it from the packaging and place it on a microwave-safe plate; microwave on 50% power 30-60 seconds or until softened.

- To slice cheesecake easily, dip a knife into a bowl of warm water before slicing each piece. This ensures the knife will glide right through. For perfect slices, wipe the knife clean after each cut.

- If you're using a recipe for baked cheesecake, prevent cracks during cooling by loosening the cake from the sides of the pan soon after baking.

✳

TEST KITCHEN TIP
When a recipe calls for beating until stiff peaks form, you should beat cream or egg whites until soft, rounded peaks appear when the beaters are lifted up.

HOW TO PIPE FROSTING

(Pictured above)

- Secure the frosting tip and coupler onto the pastry bag (or cut the corner off a food-safe plastic bag—your choice). Place the tip of the bag in a tall, empty glass. Fold the wide opening of the bag halfway over the glass. Use a spoon to transfer frosting to the bag, switching back and forth between the green and white frostings.

- When the bag is three-fourths full, pull the sides of the bag up over the frosting. Remove the bag from the glass, twist the open end to close it and apply pressure to the bag to pipe. Beautiful cupcakes, here you come!

CREME DE MENTHE CUPCAKES

*We use creme de menthe (a liqueur that means "mint cream" in French)
to add a cool touch to these impressive mascarpone-frosted cupcakes.*
—Keri Whitney, Castro Valley, CA

Prep: 30 min. **Bake:** 15 min. + cooling **Makes:** about 1 dozen

¾ cup butter, softened
1 cup granulated sugar
2 large eggs, room temperature
½ teaspoon mint extract
1½ cups cake flour
1½ teaspoons baking powder
¼ teaspoon salt
⅔ cup 2% milk
2 tablespoons white (clear) creme de menthe
Green paste food coloring

FROSTING
1 carton (8 ounces) mascarpone cheese
⅓ cup heavy whipping cream
¼ cup confectioners' sugar
4 teaspoons white (clear) creme de menthe
Green paste food coloring

1. Preheat oven to 350°. Cream butter and granulated sugar until light and fluffy. Add the eggs, one at a time, beating well after each addition. Add mint extract. In another bowl, whisk flour, baking powder and salt; add to creamed mixture alternately with milk and creme de menthe, beating well after each addition. Transfer two cups batter to a separate bowl. Mix food coloring paste into remaining batter.

2. Cut a small hole in the tip of a pastry bag or in a corner of a food-safe plastic bag; insert a #12 round tip. Spoon the batters alternately into bag. Pipe batter into 12 paper-lined muffin cups until three-fourths full. Bake until a toothpick comes out clean, 15-20 minutes. Cool 10 minutes; remove from pan to a wire rack to cool completely.

3. For frosting, stir the mascarpone and whipping cream together until smooth. Add the confectioners' sugar and the creme de menthe; stir until blended. Transfer half of the frosting to a separate bowl and mix food coloring paste into remaining frosting. Stir each portion vigorously until stiff peaks form (do not overmix).

4. Cut a small hole in the tip of a pastry bag or in a corner of a food-safe plastic bag; insert a #12 round tip. Spoon the frostings alternately into the bag. Pipe frosting onto cupcakes. Refrigerate any leftovers.

Note: For extra-thick frosting like that shown in the photo, double all frosting ingredients.

BIG & BUTTERY CHOCOLATE CHIP COOKIES

Based on a recipe from a bakery in California called Hungry Bear,
our version of the classic cookie is big, thick and chewy—perfect for dunking.
—Irene Yeh, Mequon, WI

Prep: 35 min. + chilling **Bake:** 10 min./batch **Makes:** about 2 dozen

1 cup butter, softened
1 cup packed brown sugar
¾ cup sugar
2 large eggs
1½ teaspoons vanilla extract
2⅔ cups all-purpose flour
1¼ teaspoons baking soda
1 teaspoon salt
1 package (12 ounces) semisweet chocolate chips
2 cups coarsely chopped walnuts, toasted

1. In a large bowl, beat butter and sugars until blended. Beat in eggs and vanilla. In a small bowl, whisk flour, baking soda and salt; gradually beat into butter mixture. Stir in chocolate chips and walnuts.

2. Shape ¼ cupfuls of the dough into balls. Flatten each to ¾-in. thickness (2½-in. diameter), smoothing edges as necessary. Place in an airtight container, separating the layers with waxed or parchment paper; refrigerate, covered, overnight.

3. To bake, place dough portions 2 in. apart on parchment paper-lined baking sheets; let stand at room temperature 30 minutes before baking. Preheat oven to 400°.

4. Bake 10-12 minutes or until edges are golden brown (centers will be light). Cool on pans 2 minutes. Remove to wire racks to cool.

Almond Chocolate Chip Cookies: Reduce vanilla to 1 teaspoon and add ¼ teaspoon almond extract. Substitute toasted almonds for the walnuts.

Big & Buttery White Chip Cookies: Substitute white baking chips for the chocolate chips and toasted hazelnuts for the walnuts.

Big & Buttery Cranberry Nut Cookies: Substitute dried cranberries for chocolate chips.

Big & Buttery Cherry Chocolate Chip Cookies: Substitute 1 cup of chopped dried cherries for 1 cup of the walnuts.

Note: To toast nuts, bake in a shallow pan in a 350° oven for 5-10 minutes or cook in a skillet over low heat until lightly browned, stirring occasionally.

JUST LIKE MOM'S

A MEAL WITH 5 INGREDIENTS
(OR FEWER)

◇◇◇

We've all been there: Sometimes you run low on groceries but don't feel like running to the store. It's OK! Turns out you can make an entire meal with just five ingredients (plus staples like salt, pepper, water and oil).

TURKEY-CRANBERRY BAGELS

If you don't have sliced cooked turkey available, go ahead and use some deli turkey meat. It's good with all sorts of cranberry sauces and chutneys, so have fun playing around.
—*Taste of Home* Test Kitchen

Start to Finish: 10 min. **Makes:** 4 servings

4 plain bagels, split and toasted
8 ounces thinly sliced cooked turkey
½ cup whole-berry cranberry sauce
8 slices provolone cheese

Preheat broiler. Place bagel halves on a baking sheet; layer with turkey, cranberry sauce and cheese. Broil 4-6 in. from heat 1-2 minutes or until cheese is melted.

HOW TO MAKE BAGELS AT HOME

(Pictured left, top to bottom)

You'll need:
1 tablespoon active dry yeast
1¼ cups warm water (110° to 115°)
3 tablespoons canola oil
3 tablespoons sugar
3 tablespoons plus ¼ cup honey, divided
1 teaspoon brown sugar
1½ teaspoons salt
1 large egg
4 to 5 cups bread flour
Thermometer
Large bowl
Slotted spoon
Optional toppings: minced onion, sesame seeds and poppy seeds

• In a large bowl, dissolve yeast in warm water (use thermometer to check temperature). Add the oil, sugar, 3 tablespoons honey, brown sugar, salt and egg. Mix ingredients together well, then stir in enough flour to form a soft dough. The flour will give the dough just enough binding to stick together. It should feel very pliable and give way easily in your hands.

• Turn the dough out onto a floured surface, scraping the bowl as needed, and begin to knead by hand. Press and fold the dough. As you knead it, the dough will tighten, taking on a slightly elastic feel. A visual cue that the dough is close to perfect is when it loses its matte surface and gains a subtle shine. You'll know it's done when it feels smooth and heavy in your hands. This takes 8-10 minutes of kneading. When finished, grab a tea towel and cover the dough, letting it rest for 10 minutes.

• Punch the dough down. To help prevent your hands from sticking, moisten them with water before shaping the dough. Then divvy it up and shape it into 12 balls. Use your thumb to create a hole in the center of one dough ball. The hole should be about 1½ inches wide. Next, stretch and shape the bagel into an even ring. This'll prevent it from becoming lopsided and will help it cook evenly. Repeat with the remaining dough. Place the bagels on a floured surface. Cover and let them rest for another

10 minutes. After they've rested, flatten the bagels ever so slightly with your fingertips.

• In a large saucepan or Dutch oven, bring about 8 cups of water and the remaining honey to a boil. One at a time, drop the bagels into the boiling water. You'll need to flip them soon enough, so don't overload the pot. (It's no fun trying to handle bagels in a crowded pot of scalding water.) Cook bagels for 45 seconds, then turn over and cook 45 seconds longer.

• Remove bagels from the water using a slotted spoon, allowing any extra water to drain off. Sprinkle desired seasonings on top of the bagels.

• Place the bagels about 2 inches apart on baking sheets lined with parchment paper. Bake at 425° for 12 minutes. Flip each bagel and bake 5 minutes longer or until golden brown. The end result? A dozen perfectly chewy, slightly sweet bagels.

OVEN-ROASTED ASPARAGUS

Asparagus never tasted so good! Seasoned simply with butter and green onions, they taste fresh and keep their bright green color, too. They're so good, you might want to make extra.
—Jody Fisher, Stewartstown, PA

Start to Finish: 20 min. **Makes:** 6 servings

2 **pounds fresh asparagus, trimmed**
¼ **cup butter, melted**
2 **to 4 green onions, chopped**
½ **teaspoon salt**

* See page 117 for instructions on prepping asparagus.

1. Preheat oven to 425°. Place the asparagus in a 15x10x1-in. pan. Toss with melted butter and green onions; spread evenly. Sprinkle with salt.

2. Roast until asparagus is crisp-tender, 10-15 minutes.

CHEESY CHICKEN & BROCCOLI ORZO

Broccoli and rice casserole tops my family's comfort food list, but when we need something fast, this is the stuff. Cooking chicken and veggie orzo on the stovetop speeds everything up.
—Mary Shivers, Ada, OK

Start to Finish: 30 min. **Makes:** 6 servings

1¼ cups uncooked orzo pasta
2 packages (10 ounces each) frozen broccoli with cheese sauce
2 tablespoons butter
1½ pounds boneless skinless chicken breasts, cut into ½-inch cubes
1 medium onion, chopped
¾ teaspoon salt
½ teaspoon pepper

1. Cook orzo according to package directions. Meanwhile, heat broccoli with cheese sauce according to package directions.

2. In a large skillet, heat butter over medium heat. Add chicken, onion, salt and pepper; cook and stir 6-8 minutes or until chicken is no longer pink and onion is tender. Drain orzo. Stir orzo and broccoli with cheese sauce into skillet; heat through.

✳
TEST KITCHEN TIP
Because of orzo's similar shape and mild flavor, it can be substituted for rice in many recipes. Nutritionally speaking, the two are similar.

WHY YOU'LL LOVE IT...
"Easy and delicious. Reheated well in the microwave with a few drops of water added."
—TGI, TASTEOFHOME.COM

SAUCY RANCH PORK & POTATOES

A while back, my sister Elyse shared a tasty ranch pork roast recipe. I tweaked it so I could use what was already in my pantry, and this dish was an instant win.
—Kendra Adamson, Layton, UT

Prep: 20 min. **Cook:** 4 hours **Makes:** 6 servings

- 2 pounds red potatoes (about 6 medium), cut into ¾-inch cubes
- ¼ cup water
- 6 boneless pork loin chops (6 ounces each)
- 2 cans (10¾ ounces each) condensed cream of chicken soup, undiluted
- 1 cup 2% milk
- 1 envelope ranch salad dressing mix
  Minced fresh parsley, optional

1. Place potatoes and water in a large microwave-safe dish. Microwave, covered, on high for 3-5 minutes or until potatoes are almost tender; drain.

2. Transfer potatoes and pork chops to a 4- or 5-qt. slow cooker. In a bowl, mix condensed soup, milk and salad dressing mix; pour over pork chops. Cook, covered, on low 4-5 hours or until pork and potatoes are tender (a thermometer inserted in pork should read at least 145°). If desired, sprinkle with parsley.

✳

TEST KITCHEN TIP
Before buying a bag of potatoes (or apples, oranges or onions), take a look to make sure none of them are bruised or spoiled.

SLOW-COOKED
YUM!

CHEESY CHILI FRIES

My family is all about chili fries, but restaurant versions pile on the calories.
For a healthier approach, bake them and serve with vegetarian chili and avocado.
—Beverly Nowling, Bristol, FL

Start to Finish: 30 min. **Makes:** 4 servings

5 cups frozen seasoned curly fries
1 tablespoon olive oil
1 can (15 ounces) vegetarian chili with beans
1 cup shredded cheddar cheese
    Optional toppings: sour cream, thinly sliced green onions and cubed avocado

1. Preheat oven to 450°. Place fries on an ungreased 15x10x1-in. baking pan; drizzle with oil and toss to coat. Bake according to package directions.

2. Divide fries among four 2-cup baking dishes; top each with chili and cheese. Bake 5-7 minutes or until cheese is melted. Serve with toppings as desired.

Note: You may use an 8-in. square baking dish instead of four 2-cup baking dishes. Bake as directed.

ROASTED CAULIFLOWER & BRUSSELS SPROUTS WITH BACON

Between the roasted flavor of the veggies and the crisp, smoky bacon, this delicious side dish will convert even the pickiest eater.

—Lisa Speer, Palm Beach, FL

Prep: 30 min. **Bake:** 20 min. **Makes:** 10 servings

2 pounds fresh Brussels sprouts, thinly sliced
1 pound fresh cauliflowerets (about 7 cups), thinly sliced
¼ cup olive oil
1 teaspoon freshly ground pepper
½ teaspoon salt
1 pound bacon strips, cooked and crumbled
⅓ to ½ cup balsamic vinaigrette

1. Preheat oven to 375°. In a very large bowl, toss Brussels sprouts and cauliflower with oil, pepper and salt. Transfer to two greased 15x10x1-in. baking pans.

2. Roast 20-25 minutes or until vegetables are tender. Transfer to a serving bowl. Just before serving, add bacon and drizzle with vinaigrette; toss to coat.

WHY YOU'LL LOVE IT...

"My family loved this. I even went back for more and I have never been a Brussels sprouts fan! It was equally good the next day."

—GHAUS, TASTEOFHOME.COM

S'MORES WITHOUT THE STICK!

S'MORES CRESCENT ROLLS

Here's how to score indoor s'mores: Grab crescent dough and Nutella.
—Cathy Trochelman, Brookfield, WI

Start to Finish: 25 min. **Makes:** 8 servings

1 tube (8 ounces) refrigerated crescent rolls
¼ cup Nutella, divided
2 whole graham crackers, broken up
2 tablespoons milk chocolate chips
⅔ cup miniature marshmallows

1. Preheat oven to 375°. Unroll crescent dough; separate into eight triangles. Place 1 teaspoon Nutella at the wide end of each triangle; sprinkle with graham crackers, chocolate chips and marshmallows. Roll up and place on ungreased baking sheets, point side down; curve to form crescents. Bake 9-11 minutes or until golden brown.

2. In a microwave, warm remaining Nutella to reach a drizzling consistency; spoon over rolls. Serve warm.

* Keep the summery food theme going by flipping to page 238 to discover grilled favorites.

BLUEBERRY CREAM POPS

Blueberries and cream make such a fun afternoon snack. And these are so simple to make!
—Cindy Reams, Philipsburg, PA

Prep: 15 min. + freezing **Makes:** 8 pops

⅔ cup sugar
⅔ cup water
2 cups fresh or frozen blueberries, thawed
¼ cup heavy whipping cream
8 freezer pop molds or 8 paper cups (3 ounces each) and wooden pop sticks

1. For sugar syrup, in a small saucepan, combine sugar and water; bring to a boil, stirring to dissolve sugar. Cool completely.

2. Meanwhile, in a bowl, coarsely mash blueberries; stir in cream and sugar syrup. Spoon into molds or paper cups. Top molds with holders. If using cups, top with foil and insert sticks through foil. Freeze until firm. To serve, let pops stand at room temperature 10 minutes before unmolding.

HOW TO CHOOSE A POP MOLD

- Have a specialty mold you got from the store? Great! You're on your way to becoming a frozen-pop pro.

- No kit? Don't sweat it. It's easy to form and freeze pops using everyday items for molds. Ice cube trays, small disposable cups and muffin tins lined with foil cupcake wrappers can be used in lieu of a mold. Your pops may be a little wider around, but they'll taste just as good! Simply pour the ingredients into your DIY mold, cover with foil and spear a wooden pop stick through the foil into the center of the mold. The foil will help the stick stay upright.

✳
TEST KITCHEN TIP
After pulling these frozen treats from the freezer, give them a quick dip in hot water. They'll slide right out of the mold.

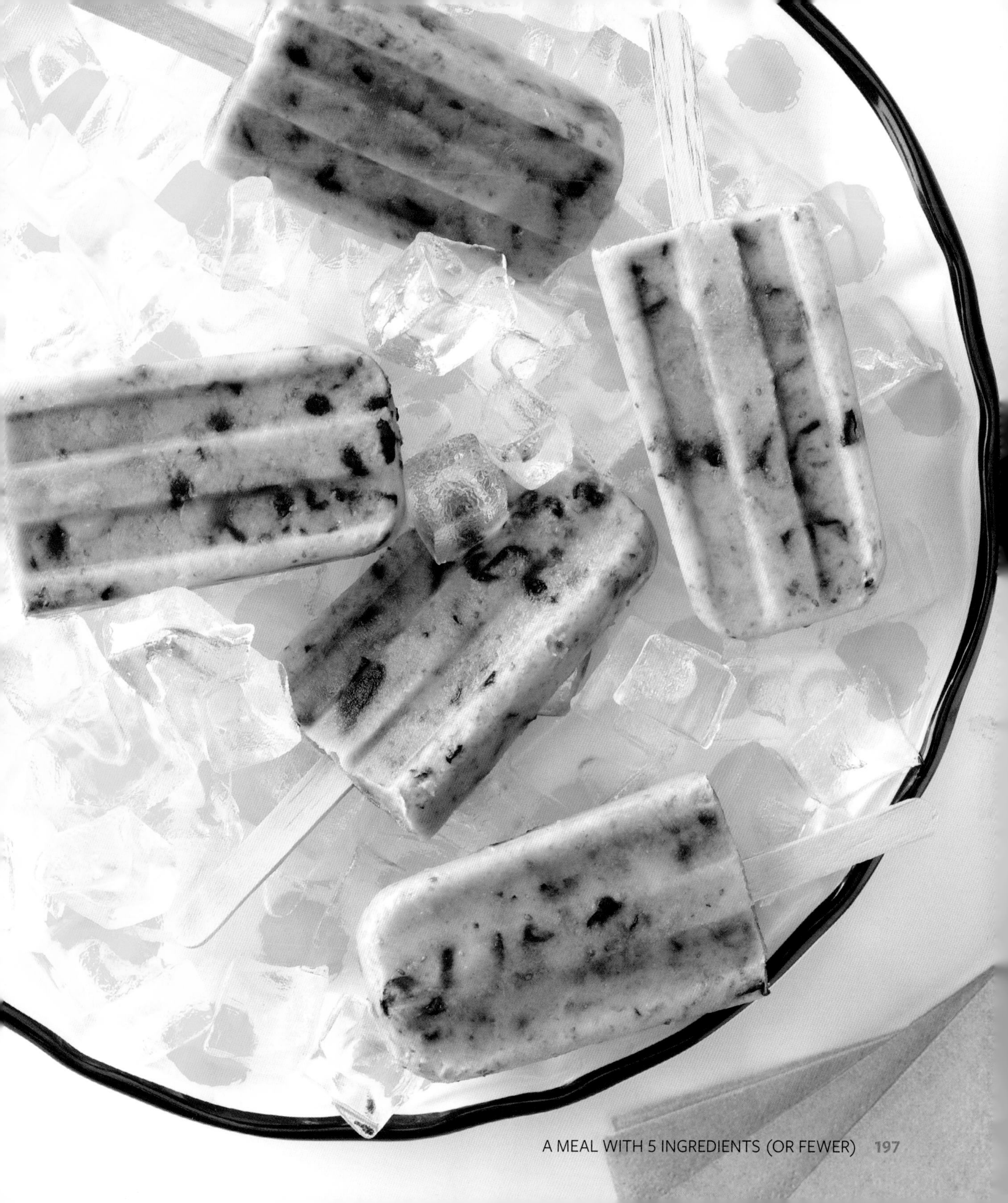

A MEAL IN 30 MINUTES
(OR LESS)

◇◇◇

Only have a half-hour to whip something up...but you're hungry now?
You're in luck! This chapter is devoted to recipes that take 30 minutes max.
There's no need for fast food when you can make food this fast.

EASY GROUND BEEF TACO SALAD

Every time I have to bring a dish to a party, friends ask for my taco salad. Players on my son's football team ask for it, too.
—Lori Buntrock, Wisconsin Rapids, WI

Start to Finish: 30 min. **Makes:** 6 servings

1 pound ground beef
1 envelope reduced-sodium taco seasoning
¾ cup water
1 medium head iceberg lettuce, torn (about 8 cups)
2 cups shredded cheddar cheese
2 cups lightly crushed nacho-flavored tortilla chips
¼ cup Catalina salad dressing

1. In a large skillet, cook beef over medium heat 6-8 minutes or until no longer pink, breaking into crumbles; drain. Stir in taco seasoning and water; bring to a boil. Reduce heat; simmer, uncovered, 4-6 minutes or until thickened, stirring occasionally. Cool slightly.

2. In a large bowl, toss lettuce with cheese. Top with beef mixture and chips; drizzle with dressing and toss to combine. Serve immediately.

※
TEST KITCHEN TIP
When buying beef, look for meat that is bright and cherry-red in color with no gray or brown patches...and a sell-by date in the future.

HOW TO MAKE RESTAURANT-STYLE SALSA

(Pictured left)

You'll need:
1 can (28 ounces) whole
tomatoes, drained
1 can (14½ ounces) diced
tomatoes with garlic and
onion, drained
1 can (14½ ounces) Mexican
stewed tomatoes, drained
1 can (10 ounces) diced
tomatoes and green chilies,
drained
1 medium onion, quartered
2 banana peppers, seeded
and coarsely chopped
2 jalapeno peppers, seeded and
coarsely chopped
3 garlic cloves, minced
2 teaspoons salt
¼ teaspoon ground cumin
½ cup minced fresh cilantro
¼ cup lime juice
2 medium ripe avocados, peeled
and cubed
Tortilla chips

• This part is easy! Place the
first 10 ingredients in a food
processor; let the processor
do the hard work until all the
ingredients are chopped. Add
cilantro and lime juice; cover
and pulse until combined.

• Transfer to a bowl; stir in
avocados. Serve with tortilla
chips or on top of taco salad
for a bit of spice!

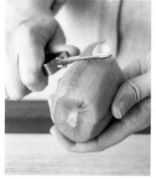

HOW TO PEEL A KIWI

(Pictured above)

- Option A is to cut both ends from fruit. Using a spoon, scoop out the flesh. Cut into slices, wedges or chunks with a sharp knife.

- Option B also begins with cutting both ends from the fruit. Using a vegetable peeler, peel off the fuzzy brown skin. Cut as above.

FRESH FRUIT COMBO

Whenever I take this eye-catching fruit salad to a party or gathering, people ask for the recipe. The blueberries and cherries give the salad its distinctive flavor.
—Julie Sterchi, Campbellsville, KY

Start to Finish: 20 min. **Makes:** 14 servings

2 cups cubed fresh pineapple
2 medium oranges, peeled and chopped
3 kiwifruit, peeled and sliced
1 cup sliced fresh strawberries
1 cup halved seedless red grapes
2 medium firm bananas, sliced
1 large red apple, cubed
1 cup fresh or frozen blueberries
1 cup fresh or canned pitted dark sweet cherries

In a large bowl, combine the first five ingredients; refrigerate until serving. Just before serving, fold in the bananas, apple, blueberries and cherries.

BLACK BEAN TURKEY CHILI

This busy-day chili is packed with flavor. We make it ahead and freeze some to eat later.
—Marisela Segovia, Miami, FL

Start to Finish: 30 min. **Makes:** 6 servings

1 pound lean ground turkey
1 large green pepper, chopped
1 medium onion, chopped
2 tablespoons chili powder
½ teaspoon salt
¼ teaspoon pepper
⅛ to ¼ teaspoon cayenne pepper
1 can (15 ounces) no-salt-added tomato sauce
1 can (15 ounces) black beans, rinsed and drained
1½ cups frozen corn (about 8 ounces), thawed
1 large tomato, chopped
½ cup water
Shredded cheddar cheese, optional

1. In a 6-qt. stockpot, cook and crumble turkey with green pepper and onion over medium-high heat until no longer pink, 5-7 minutes. Stir in the seasonings; cook 1 minute.

2. Stir in tomato sauce, beans, corn, tomato and water; bring to a boil. Reduce heat; simmer, uncovered, to allow flavors to blend, about 10 minutes, stirring occasionally. If desired, serve with cheese.

To freeze: Freeze cooled chili in freezer containers. To use, partially thaw in refrigerator overnight. Heat through in a saucepan, stirring occasionally and adding a little water if necessary.

* Corn bread goes great with this chili. Turn to page 57 for a recipe we love.

PASTA WITH ROASTED GARLIC & TOMATOES

Here's a simple sauce with just four ingredients, and it's nice enough for a party. I use bow tie pasta, but penne works, too.
—Aysha Schurman, Ammon, ID

Start to Finish: 20 min. **Makes:** 4 servings

1½ pounds cherry tomatoes
12 garlic cloves, peeled
3 tablespoons olive oil
3 cups uncooked bow tie pasta
4 ounces (½ cup) cream cheese, softened
½ teaspoon salt

1. Preheat oven to 450°. In a bowl, toss tomatoes and garlic cloves with oil; transfer to a greased 15x10x1-in. baking pan. Roast 14-16 minutes or until very soft. Meanwhile, cook pasta according to package directions.

2. Cool tomato mixture slightly. Reserve 12 tomatoes for serving with pasta. Transfer remaining tomato mixture to a food processor. Add cream cheese and salt; process until smooth. Transfer to a large bowl.

3. Drain pasta; add to tomato mixture and toss to coat. Top with reserved tomatoes.

WHY YOU'LL LOVE IT...

"My family really enjoyed this recipe! The cream cheese is a nice change in flavor for a tomato-based recipe and creates an appealing creamy texture. I used Neufchatel cream cheese to cut down on the fat. I will add this to my frequently used pasta dish recipes."
—DDB88, TASTEOFHOME.COM

MUFFIN TIN LASAGNAS

This is a fun way to serve lasagna and a great way to surprise everyone at the table. Quick and versatile, these little cups can be made with the ingredients your family likes best.
—Sally Kilkenny, Granger, IA

Start to Finish: 30 min. **Makes:** 6 servings

1 large egg, lightly beaten
1 carton (15 ounces) part-skim ricotta cheese
2 cups shredded Italian cheese blend, divided
1 tablespoon olive oil
24 wonton wrappers
1 jar (24 ounces) garden-style pasta sauce
  Minced fresh parsley, optional

1. Preheat oven to 375°. In a bowl, mix egg, ricotta cheese and 1¼ cups Italian cheese blend.

2. Generously grease 12 muffin cups with oil; line each with a wonton wrapper. Fill each with 1 tablespoon ricotta mixture and 1½ tablespoons pasta sauce. Top each with a second wrapper, rotating corners and pressing down centers. Repeat ricotta and sauce layers. Sprinkle with the remaining cheese blend.

3. Bake 20-25 minutes or until the cheese is melted. If desired, sprinkle with parsley.

HOW TO MAKE HOMEMADE RICOTTA

(Pictured bottom right, left to right)

You'll need:
2 quarts whole milk
1 cup heavy whipping cream
½ teaspoon salt
3 tablespoons white vinegar
Strainer inside another bowl and with two layers of cheese cloth over top

Test Kitchen tip: The milk needs to separate into curds and whey, so you actually need fat to make ricotta. It's important to use milk with a higher fat content. Whole or 2% will do the trick.

- To make ricotta, start by straining the whey and collecting the curds. Get your setup together. First, line a large strainer with two layers of cheesecloth dampened with water. This creates a superfine filter for the ricotta mixture. Next, place the strainer over a large bowl.

- Time to cook! In a Dutch oven, bring the milk, cream and salt just to a boil over medium heat. Stir the mixture occasionally to prevent scorching. Once it's bubbling, remove from the heat and gently stir in the vinegar. Then step away and let the mixture stand, allowing time for the curds to form. This should take about 5 minutes. In the meantime, resist the urge to poke or stir.

- Slowly pour the curdled mixture into the cheesecloth strainer. It will drain slowly, anywhere from 30 minutes to an hour. What's left in the strainer—soft curds of lightly tangy cheese—is the ricotta. Its consistency should be soft and spreadable but not watery. (If it's watery, let it strain a while longer.)

Put leftovers in the fridge. Chilled, ricotta will last for about 5 days.

Test Kitchen tip: Don't discard the strained liquid. It's whey—and though you can drink it, most people like to use it in baked goods like muffins or sourdough, where it provides a tang akin to buttermilk.

GRILLED GARDEN VEGGIE PIZZA

Pile on the veggies! This crisp grilled crust can take it. My colorful, healthy pizza looks as fresh as it tastes.
—Diane Halferty, Corpus Christi, TX

Start to Finish: 30 min. **Makes:** 6 servings

1 medium red onion, cut crosswise into ½-inch slices
1 large sweet red pepper, halved, stemmed and seeded
1 small zucchini, cut lengthwise into ½-inch slices
1 yellow summer squash, cut lengthwise into ½-inch slices
2 tablespoons olive oil
½ teaspoon salt
¼ teaspoon pepper
1 prebaked 12-inch thin whole wheat pizza crust
3 tablespoons jarred roasted minced garlic
2 cups shredded part-skim mozzarella cheese, divided
⅓ cup torn fresh basil

1. Brush the vegetables with oil; sprinkle with salt and pepper. Grill, covered, over medium heat until tender, 4-5 minutes per side for onion and pepper, 3-4 minutes per side for zucchini and squash.

2. Separate onion into rings; cut pepper into strips. Spread pizza crust with garlic; sprinkle with 1 cup cheese. Top with grilled vegetables, then top with remaining cheese.

3. Grill pizza, covered, over medium heat until the bottom is golden brown and cheese is melted, 5-7 minutes. Top with basil.

*

TEST KITCHEN TIP
Did you know? There are more than 30 varieties of basil, but sweet basil is the most commonly used.

CRISPY FISH & CHIPS

A British pub classic gets upscale when you add horseradish, panko and Worcestershire sauce. You can also try it with a white fish such as cod or haddock.
—Linda Schend, Kenosha, WI

Start to Finish: 30 min. **Makes:** 4 servings

4 cups frozen steak fries
4 salmon fillets (6 ounces each)
1 to 2 tablespoons prepared horseradish
1 tablespoon grated Parmesan cheese
1 tablespoon Worcestershire sauce
1 teaspoon Dijon mustard
¼ teaspoon salt
½ cup panko (Japanese) bread crumbs
Cooking spray

1. Preheat oven to 450°. Arrange steak fries in a single layer on a baking sheet. Bake on lowest oven rack 18-20 minutes or until light golden brown.

2. Meanwhile, place salmon on a foil-lined baking sheet coated with cooking spray. In a small bowl, mix horseradish, cheese, Worcestershire sauce, mustard and salt; stir in panko. Press mixture onto fillets. Spritz tops with cooking spray.

3. Bake salmon on middle oven rack 8-10 minutes or until fish just begins to flake easily with a fork. Serve with fries.

WHY YOU'LL LOVE IT...

"Absolutely delicious! Loved the crunchy coating. I substituted sweet potato fries for the steak fries and sprinkled malt vinegar on both my fish and chips."

—LMMANDA, TASTEOFHOME.COM

DIY FRIDAY FISH FRY!

✳

TEST KITCHEN TIP
When preparing rice for a recipe, make some extra for a busy day! Cooked rice can be refrigerated for several days. To reheat rice, add 2 tablespoons of liquid for each cup of rice. Cook in a saucepan or microwave in a microwave-safe bowl until heated through.

ASIAN CHICKEN RICE BOWL

This nutrient-packed dish makes use of supermarket conveniences like coleslaw mix and rotisserie chicken. The recipe is easily doubled or tripled for large families.
—Christianna Gozzi, Astoria, NY

Start to Finish: 20 min. **Makes:** 4 servings

¼ cup rice vinegar
1 green onion, minced
2 tablespoons reduced-sodium soy sauce
1 tablespoon toasted sesame seeds
1 tablespoon sesame oil
1 tablespoon honey
1 teaspoon minced fresh gingerroot

1 package (8.8 ounces) ready-to-serve brown rice
4 cups coleslaw mix (about 9 ounces)
2 cups shredded rotisserie chicken, chilled
2 cups frozen shelled edamame, thawed

1. For dressing, whisk together first seven ingredients. Cook rice according to package directions. Divide among four bowls.

2. In a large bowl, toss coleslaw mix and chicken with half of the dressing. Serve edamame and slaw mixture over rice; drizzle with remaining dressing.

HOW TO COOK BROWN RICE

(Pictured bottom left)

Rice is one of the most versatile players in a mealtime lineup. It's also one of the simplest to make. Our foolproof guide will teach you how to cook brown rice, with helpful tips along the way.

You'll need:
Small saucepan with lid
Measuring cups
Liquid—usually water
Brown rice

Note: These steps are designed for cooking long grain brown rice. If you've picked up a package of instant, jump to the end for some alternative tips.

• First thing's first: Figure out how much rice to use. The math is super easy. We like to remember it as 1-2-3:

1 cup uncooked rice +
2 cups liquid =
3 cups cooked rice

Notice we said liquid? Water is perfectly fine, but if you're looking to jazz up a dish, you can replace some or all of the water with broth or light coconut milk. Just make sure to keep the rice-to-liquid ratio the same.

And what about rinsing? By and large, it isn't necessary. If rinsing or soaking is required, this information will be included on the package or in the recipe.

• After placing the rice and liquid into a small saucepan, crank up the heat. Bring the contents of the pot to a nice bubbling boil. They say a watched pot never boils, but in this case, it's best to keep an eye on it.

• Once the water begins to boil, reduce the heat. Cover the saucepan and let it simmer for 35-45 minutes. It's OK if you want to take the lid off and peek in every once in a while. Rice is done when its texture is tender and the liquid has been absorbed.
Test Kitchen tip: If the cooking liquid is nearly gone and the rice isn't tender yet, add a little more liquid to help it finish cooking.

A note on cooking instant rice:
Don't feel guilty for grabbing a package of the instant stuff. Quick and instant brown rices are just as healthy as regular, and they cook in as few as 10 minutes—a welcome shortcut in any kitchen. Just follow the instructions on the box. These rices have been partially cooked and dehydrated, so they require different ratios than standard rice.

HEAVENLY FILLED STRAWBERRIES

These luscious stuffed berries are the perfect bite-sized dessert.
—Stephen Munro, Beaverbank, NS

Start to Finish: 20 min. **Makes:** 3 dozen

3 dozen large fresh strawberries
11 ounces cream cheese, softened
½ cup confectioners' sugar
¼ teaspoon almond extract
   Grated chocolate, optional

1. Remove stems from strawberries; cut a deep "X" in the tip of each berry. Gently spread berries open.

2. In a small bowl, beat the cream cheese, confectioners' sugar and extract until light and fluffy. Pipe or spoon about 2 teaspoons into each berry; if desired, sprinkle with chocolate. Chill until serving.

HOW TO QUICKLY HULL A STRAWBERRY

Insert a drinking straw into the tip of the berry and push the hull through the other end.

✳
TEST KITCHEN TIP
Strawberries peak between April and June, so pick them at their freshest and enjoy this recipe!

HOW DO I MAKE...

A HEALTHY MEAL

◊◊◊

It's time for some good-for-you eats. Start your day with a strata packed
with veggies, wow friends with DIY tomato sauce (no cooking involved!)
or discover a new, light dinner favorite. Eating right starts here!

CUCUMBER BOATS

*I've had a garden for decades, and these colorful boats made from cucumbers
hold my fresh tomatoes, peas and dill. It's absolute garden greatness.*
—Ronna Farley, Rockville, MD

Start to Finish: 15 min. **Makes:** 2 servings

2 medium cucumbers
½ cup fat-free plain Greek yogurt
2 tablespoons mayonnaise
½ teaspoon garlic salt
3 teaspoons snipped fresh dill, divided
1 cup chopped cooked chicken breast
1 cup chopped seeded tomato (about 1 large), divided
½ cup fresh or frozen peas, thawed

1. Cut each cucumber lengthwise in half; scoop out pulp, leaving a ¼-in. shell. In a bowl, mix yogurt, mayonnaise, garlic salt and 1 teaspoon dill; gently stir in chicken, ¾ cup tomato and peas.

2. Spoon into cucumber shells. Top with the remaining tomato and dill.

✳

TEST KITCHEN TIP
When purchasing bags of frozen vegetables, such as peas, examine the packages for signs that they've been thawed and refrozen. Steer clear of vegetables that are frozen in blocks or large chunks. If the packages are transparent, check for crystallization. Both indicate thawing and refreezing, which can diminish quality.

NO GLUTEN HERE!

GLUTEN-FREE CHILI BEEF PASTA

After I got married, my aunt gave me her recipe for skillet spaghetti and told me it was ideal for a quick weeknight meal. Over the years I've changed up the ingredients and played with the seasonings to make it healthier. It's a dish my family truly loves.
—Kristen Killian, Depew, NY

Start to Finish: 30 min. **Makes:** 6 servings

1 pound lean ground beef (90% lean)
2 tablespoons dried minced onion
2 teaspoons dried oregano
2 teaspoons chili powder
½ teaspoon garlic powder
⅛ teaspoon salt
3 cups tomato juice
2 cups water
1 can (6 ounces) tomato paste
1 teaspoon sugar
8 ounces uncooked gluten-free spiral pasta
  Chopped tomatoes and minced fresh oregano, optional

1. In a Dutch oven, cook beef over medium heat 6-8 minutes or until no longer pink, breaking into crumbles; drain. Stir in seasonings.

2. Add tomato juice, water, tomato paste and sugar to pan; bring to a boil. Stir in pasta. Reduce heat; simmer, covered, 20-22 minutes or until pasta is tender, stirring occasionally. If desired, top with tomatoes and oregano.

✳

TEST KITCHEN TIP
Defrosting ground beef that's been living in the freezer? Move it to the refrigerator 24 hours before you plan on cooking, so the meat has time to fully defrost. If you're pressed for time, the microwave's defrost setting can help.

VIBRANT BLACK-EYED PEA SALAD

My black-eyed pea salad reminds me of a Southern cooking class my husband and I took while visiting Savannah, Georgia. People go nuts for it at picnics and potlucks.
—Danielle Ulam, Sewickley, PA

Prep: 25 min. + chilling **Makes:** 10 servings

2 cans (15½ ounces each) black-eyed peas, rinsed and drained
2 cups grape tomatoes, halved
1 each small green, yellow and red peppers, finely chopped
1 small red onion, chopped
1 celery rib, chopped
2 tablespoons minced fresh basil

DRESSING
¼ cup red wine vinegar or balsamic vinegar
1 tablespoon stone-ground mustard
1 teaspoon minced fresh oregano or ¼ teaspoon dried oregano
¾ teaspoon salt
½ teaspoon freshly ground pepper
¼ cup olive oil

1. In a large bowl, combine peas, tomatoes, peppers, onion, celery and basil.

2. For dressing, in a small bowl, whisk vinegar, mustard, oregano, salt and pepper. Gradually whisk in oil until blended. Drizzle over salad; toss to coat. Refrigerate, covered, at least 3 hours before serving.

WHY YOU'LL LOVE IT...
"Loved this as a dip for tortilla chips. I served with sour cream; some jalapenos might have kicked it up a notch."
—AUG2295, TASTEOFHOME.COM

LEMON PEPPER ROASTED BROCCOLI

Fresh green broccoli turns tangy and tasty when roasted with lemon juice and pepper. A sprinkle of almonds adds crunch.
—Liz Bellville, Jacksonville, NC

Start to Finish: 25 min. **Makes:** 8 servings

1½ pounds fresh broccoli florets
　　(about 12 cups)
2　tablespoons olive oil
½　teaspoon lemon juice
¼　teaspoon salt
¼　teaspoon coarsely ground pepper,
　　divided
¼　cup chopped almonds
2　teaspoons grated lemon peel

1. Preheat oven to 450°. Place broccoli in a large bowl. Whisk oil, lemon juice, salt and ⅛ teaspoon pepper until blended; drizzle over the broccoli and toss to coat. Transfer to a 15x10x1-in. baking pan.

2. Roast 10-15 minutes or until tender. Transfer to a serving dish. Sprinkle with almonds, lemon peel and remaining pepper; toss to combine.

✳

TEST KITCHEN TIP
Zest is the grated outer peel or rind of a citrus fruit (not including the bitter white membrane attached to the fruit). To remove the zest, peel thin strips with a small sharp knife, being careful not to include the white membrane, and mince finely. You can also take the whole fruit and rub it over a hand grater or Microplane.

AVOCADO & CHICKPEAS QUINOA SALAD

This delicious salad is high in protein and holds well in the fridge for a few days.
If you make it ahead, wait until right before serving to add the avocados and tomatoes.
—Elizabeth Bennett, Seattle, WA

Prep: 25 min. **Cook:** 15 min. **Makes:** 6 servings

- 1 cup quinoa, rinsed
- 1 can (15 ounces) garbanzo beans or chickpeas, rinsed and drained
- 2 cups cherry tomatoes, halved
- 1 cup crumbled feta cheese
- ½ medium ripe avocado, peeled and cubed
- 4 green onions, chopped (about ½ cup)

DRESSING
- 3 tablespoons white wine vinegar
- 1 teaspoon Dijon mustard
- ¼ teaspoon kosher salt
- ¼ teaspoon garlic powder
- ¼ teaspoon freshly ground pepper
- ¼ cup olive oil

1. Cook quinoa according to package directions; transfer to a large bowl and cool slightly.

2. Add chickpeas, tomatoes, cheese, avocado and green onions to quinoa; gently stir to combine. In a small bowl, whisk the first five dressing ingredients. Gradually whisk in oil until blended. Drizzle over salad; gently toss to coat. Refrigerate leftovers.

Note: Look for quinoa in the cereal, rice or organic food aisle.

✳ TEST KITCHEN TIP
Because kosher salt is coarser and more voluminous than table salt, they're not interchangeable in every recipe.

LIGHT &
REFRESHING

BAKED CHICKEN CHALUPAS

I wanted an easy alternative to deep-fried chalupas, so I bake the tortillas and filling, then top it all off with crunchy cabbage.
—Magdalena Flores, Abilene, TX

Prep: 20 min. **Bake:** 15 min. **Makes:** 6 servings

6 corn tortillas (6 inches)
2 teaspoons olive oil
¾ cup shredded part-skim
    mozzarella cheese
2 cups chopped cooked chicken
    breast
1 can (14½ ounces) diced tomatoes
    with mild green chilies, undrained
1 teaspoon garlic powder
1 teaspoon onion powder
1 teaspoon ground cumin
¼ teaspoon salt
¼ teaspoon pepper
½ cup finely shredded cabbage

1. Preheat oven to 350°. Place tortillas on an ungreased baking sheet. Brush each tortilla with oil; sprinkle with mozzarella cheese.

2. Place chicken, tomatoes and seasonings in a large skillet; cook and stir over medium heat 6-8 minutes or until most of the liquid is evaporated. Spoon over tortillas. Bake chalupas for 15-18 minutes or until tortillas are crisp and cheese is melted. Top with cabbage.

HOW TO COOK CHICKEN BREASTS IN A PAN
(Pictured left, top to bottom)

- Between sheets of plastic wrap, pound chicken with a meat mallet to ½-in. thickness. Since chicken breasts tend to be thin at one end and thick at the other, pounding them helps even them out and ensures more uniform cooking.

- Cook chicken for 5-6 minutes on each side. Keep the heat at medium and no higher. In a too-hot pan, the outside will cook and brown quickly while the inside may still be raw. Moderate heat helps the chicken cook gently and evenly.

- After cooking on both sides, use a thermometer to check the temp. If it says 165°, you're good to go! If not, keep cooking for a few more minutes and check again.

* Want to top your chalupas with some homemade salsa? Flip to page 201 and learn how.

ROASTED VEGETABLE STRATA

With the abundance of zucchini my garden offers in the fall, this is the perfect dish to use up what we have. Cheesy and rich, this warm, classic breakfast dish is sure to please!
—Colleen Doucette, Truro, NS

Prep: 55 min. + chilling **Bake:** 40 min. **Makes:** 8 servings

- 3 large zucchini, halved lengthwise and cut into ¾-inch slices
- 1 each medium red, yellow and orange peppers, cut into 1-inch pieces
- 2 tablespoons olive oil
- 1 teaspoon dried oregano
- ½ teaspoon salt
- ½ teaspoon pepper
- ½ teaspoon dried basil
- 1 medium tomato, chopped
- 1 loaf (1 pound) unsliced crusty Italian bread
- ½ cup shredded sharp cheddar cheese
- ½ cup shredded Asiago cheese
- 6 large eggs
- 2 cups fat-free milk

1. Preheat oven to 400°. Toss zucchini and peppers with oil and seasonings; transfer to a 15x10x1-in. pan. Roast until tender, 25-30 minutes, stirring once. Stir in tomato; cool slightly.

2. Trim ends from bread; cut bread into 1-in. slices. In a greased 13x9-in. baking dish, layer half of each of the following: bread, roasted vegetables and cheeses. Repeat layers. Whisk together eggs and milk; pour evenly over top. Refrigerate, covered, 6 hours or overnight.

3. Preheat oven to 375°. Remove casserole from refrigerator while oven heats. Bake, uncovered, until golden brown, 40-50 minutes. Let stand for 5-10 minutes before cutting.

To freeze: Cover and freeze unbaked casserole. To use, partially thaw in refrigerator overnight. Remove from the refrigerator 30 minutes before baking. Preheat oven to 375°. Bake casserole as directed, increasing time as necessary to heat through and for a thermometer inserted in center to read 165°.

ROASTED CHICKEN THIGHS WITH PEPPERS & POTATOES

My family loves this dish! It looks and tastes really special, but it is quite simple to make. It uses olive oil and the fresh herbs from my garden.
—Pattie Prescott, Manchester, NH

Prep: 20 min. **Bake:** 35 min. **Makes:** 8 servings

2 pounds red potatoes (about 6 medium)
2 large sweet red peppers
2 large green peppers
2 medium onions
2 tablespoons olive oil, divided
4 teaspoons minced fresh thyme or 1½ teaspoons dried thyme, divided
3 teaspoons minced fresh rosemary or 1 teaspoon dried rosemary, crushed, divided
8 boneless skinless chicken thighs (about 2 pounds)
½ teaspoon salt
¼ teaspoon pepper

1. Preheat oven to 450°. Cut potatoes, peppers and onions into 1-in. pieces. Place the vegetables in a roasting pan. Drizzle with 1 tablespoon oil; sprinkle with 2 teaspoons each fresh thyme and rosemary and toss to coat. Place chicken over vegetables. Brush the chicken with remaining oil; sprinkle with remaining thyme and rosemary. Sprinkle vegetables and chicken with salt and pepper.

2. Roast 35-40 minutes or until a thermometer inserted in the chicken reads 170° and vegetables are tender.

WHY YOU'LL LOVE IT...
"Delicious meal! I followed the recipe and added carrots. Will be making this again."
—MUMSAY, TASTEOFHOME.COM

NO-COOK FRESH TOMATO SAUCE

Try this sauce when you have a box of pasta or a store-bought pizza shell and need a fresh topping. Dinner is served!
—Julianne Schnuck, Milwaukee, WI

Prep: 15 min. + standing **Makes:** about 3½ cups

1½ pounds assorted fresh tomatoes, coarsely chopped (about 4½ cups)
⅓ cup minced fresh basil
1 tablespoon olive oil
2 garlic cloves, coarsely chopped
Salt and pepper to taste
Hot cooked angel hair pasta or spaghetti
Grated Parmesan cheese

1. Place tomatoes in a large bowl; stir in basil, oil and garlic. Season with salt and pepper to taste. Let stand at room temperature until juices are released from tomatoes, 30-60 minutes, stirring occasionally.

2. Serve with hot pasta. Sprinkle with Parmesan cheese.

* See page 146 for a tutorial on making zucchini noodles—perfect for serving with this homemade tomato sauce.

HOW TO WASH VEGETABLES FROM YOUR FARMERS MARKET HAUL

Avoid food poisoning. Get rid of pesky garden bugs. These are just two of the reasons we need to wash vegetables before eating them. Here are four good methods to get the job done.

Rinse in cold running water.
Best for: delicate produce

After washing your hands with warm water and soap, gather the vegetables and cut off any visibly damaged areas with a sharp knife. We know it's tempting, but don't peel the veggies just yet—simply rinse them under cold water in a sink, rubbing each section gently. Once you've patted the vegetables dry with a paper towel, you're free to peel and prepare them any way you'd like. If the veggies are tightly packed, like those delicious cherry tomatoes you couldn't resist snatching up, be sure to rinse each one.

Soak.
Best for: tightly packed, unevenly textured vegetables

Reaching every nook and cranny seems next to impossible with broccoli, cauliflower and other farmers market finds that sport a rough, bumpy texture. Here's how to do it: Fill a large pot with cool water. Add the vegetables and turn each one so every inch gets wet. Allow them to collectively soak for about two minutes, then rinse each one thoroughly to ensure that any lingering dirt particles and contaminants hiding in the veggies' exteriors are washed away completely. Never soak porous vegetables like mushrooms.

Scrub with a vegetable brush.
Best for: firm vegetables

The sturdier the veggie, the easier it is to scrape away leftover residue from pesticides. Using a produce brush, scrub cucumbers, squash, potatoes and other types of firm vegetables while simultaneously rinsing them in cold water. Once they're all clean, blot dry with a cloth. The bristles of a vegetable brush also work to remove any bugs, which is most definitely an incentive.

Wash vegetables with a white vinegar solution.
Best for: any veggie begging for a deep clean

Vegetables are pretty low-maintenance. Most of the time, they can be disinfected with water alone. In fact, the Food and Drug Administration advises against the use of detergents, soaps or any other commercial product for cleaning veggies. However, if you are extra-wary of getting a foodborne illness from contaminated vegetables, you can use a homemade white vinegar solution to sterilize. Combine 1½ cups water with ½ cup white vinegar and a teaspoon of lemon juice. Soak or spray veggies with the mixture, and dry with a clean towel. The acidic cleaner is effective and completely safe.

A MEAL ON THE GRILL

Become a grill master—we'll show you how! Inside you'll find step-by-step instructions for getting the grill hot, prepping food and making deliciously flame-kissed dishes. Get ready to claim the best-BBQ crown.

GRILLED PINEAPPLE WITH LIME DIP

Serve this dish as an appetizer or dessert—the choice is yours! If desired, the pineapple spears can be rolled in flaked coconut before grilling.
—*Taste of Home* Test Kitchen

Prep: 20 min. + marinating **Grill:** 10 min. **Makes:** 8 servings

1 fresh pineapple
¼ cup packed brown sugar
3 tablespoons honey
2 tablespoons lime juice
LIME DIP
3 ounces cream cheese, softened
¼ cup plain yogurt
2 tablespoons honey
1 tablespoon brown sugar
1 tablespoon lime juice
1 teaspoon grated lime zest

1. Peel and core the pineapple; cut into eight wedges. Cut each wedge into two spears. In a large resealable plastic bag, combine the brown sugar, honey and lime juice; add pineapple. Seal bag and turn to coat; refrigerate for 1 hour.

2. In a small bowl, beat cream cheese until smooth. Beat in the yogurt, honey, brown sugar, lime juice and zest. Cover and refrigerate until serving.

3. Coat grill rack with cooking spray before starting the grill. Drain and discard marinade. Grill pineapple, covered, over medium heat for 3-4 minutes on each side or until golden brown. Serve with lime dip.

HOW TO CUT UP A PINEAPPLE

- With a chef's knife, remove the crown and the base. Stand the pineapple upright and cut down the length to remove the eyes and rind in strips.

- Cut pineapple into quarters or as the recipe directs; cut away the core.

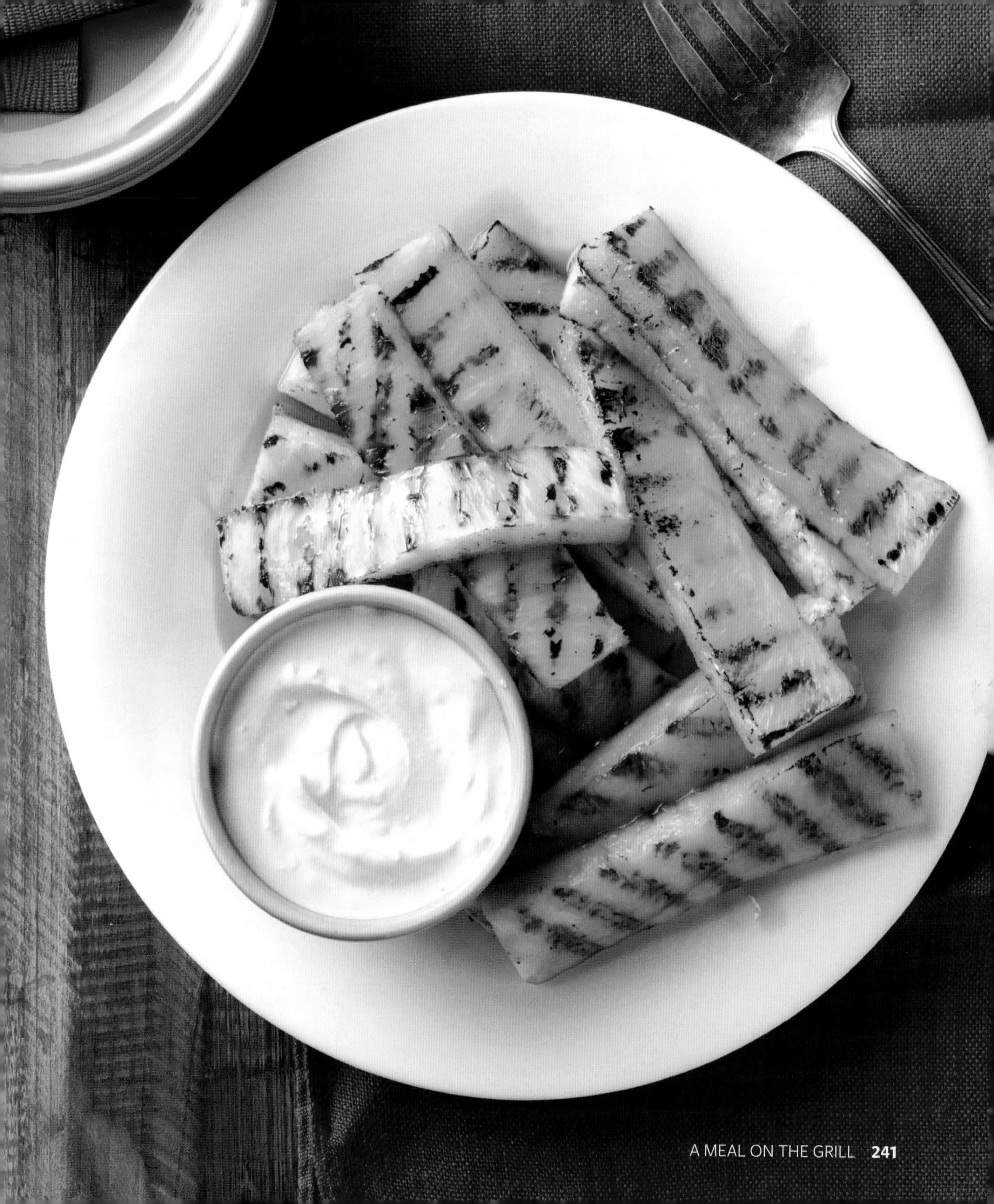

GRILLED FIRECRACKER POTATO SALAD

I can eat potato salad like crazy. A little spice is nice, so I use cayenne and paprika in this grilled salad that comes with its own fireworks.
—Ashley Armstrong, Kingsland, GA

Prep: 20 min. **Grill:** 20 min. + chilling **Makes:** 16 servings (1 cup each)

3 pounds small red potatoes (about 30), quartered
2 tablespoons olive oil
1 teaspoon salt
½ teaspoon pepper

DRESSING

1½ cups mayonnaise
½ cup finely chopped onion
¼ cup Dijon mustard
2 tablespoons sweet pickle relish
½ teaspoon paprika
¼ teaspoon cayenne pepper

SALAD

6 hard-boiled large eggs, chopped
2 celery ribs, finely chopped
Minced fresh chives, optional

1. Toss potatoes with oil, salt and pepper; place in a grill wok or basket. Grill, covered, over medium heat for 20-25 minutes or until potatoes are tender, stirring occasionally. Transfer potatoes to a large bowl; cool slightly.

2. In a small bowl, mix dressing ingredients. Add dressing, eggs and celery to potatoes; toss to combine. Refrigerate, covered, 1-2 hours or until cold. If desired, sprinkle with chives.

Note: If you do not have a grill wok or basket, use a large disposable foil pan and poke holes in the bottom of pan.

HOW TO LIGHT A CHARCOAL GRILL

There are several methods for starting a charcoal grill. Pick the one you're most comfortable with.

Chimney starter: Crumple waxed paper or newspaper into bottom of a chimney starter and place starter in the grill. Fill starter with briquettes, then light the paper. When coals are ready, dump them out of the chimney starter and spread out. Replace grill rack. This is the preferred method of *Taste of Home* Test Kitchen cooks.

Electric starter: Arrange briquettes in a pyramid in the grill. Insert starter in the middle of the coals. Plug starter into an outlet. If using an extension cord, use a heavy-duty one. It will take 8 to 10 minutes for ash to form on the coals. At that point, unplug the electric starter and remove from briquettes. The starter will be very hot, so place it out of the way on a heatproof surface. Heat briquettes until they are covered with a light gray ash. Replace grill rack.

Pyramid-style: Arrange briquettes in a pyramid in the grill. Pour lighter fluid over briquettes. Recap the fluid and place away from grill, then light the briquettes. When they're covered with light gray ash, replace grill rack.

CORN ON THE COB WITH LEMON-PEPPER BUTTER

Roasting fresh-picked corn is as old as the Ozark hills where I was raised. My Grandpa Mitchell always salted and peppered his butter on the edge of his plate before spreading it on his corn, and I did the same as a kid. Today, I continue the tradition by serving lemon-pepper butter with roasted corn—it's a favorite!
—Allene Bary-Cooper, Wichita Falls, TX

Prep: 10 min. + soaking **Grill:** 25 min. **Makes:** 8 servings

8 medium ears sweet corn
1 cup butter, softened
2 tablespoons lemon-pepper seasoning

1. Carefully peel back corn husks to within 1 in. of bottoms; remove silk. Rewrap corn in husks; secure with kitchen string. Place in a stockpot; cover with cold water. Soak 20 minutes; drain.

2. Meanwhile, in a small bowl, mix butter and lemon-pepper. Grill corn, covered, over medium heat for 20-25 minutes or until tender, turning often.

3. Cut string and peel back husks. Serve corn with butter mixture.

HOW DO YOU KNOW WHEN THE COALS ARE READY?

Get a feel for things! Cautiously hold your hand 4 inches over the coals. Start counting the number of seconds you can hold your hand in place before the heat forces you to pull away.

- If you can hold your hand above the fire for no more than 2 seconds, the heat level is "hot" (about 500°).

- If you can only hold your hand above the coals for 3 seconds, the heat level is "medium-hot" (about 400°).

- If you can hold your hand above the coals for no more than 4 seconds, the heat level is "medium" (about 350°).

- If you can hold your hand above the coals for 5 seconds, the heat level is "low" (about 300°).

✳

TEST KITCHEN TIP
Kitchen string (sometimes called kitchen twine) is worth buying. Regular string is sometimes coated with plastic, which can catch on fire or melt—and which isn't safe to eat. Stay safe and buy cotton kitchen string online, or find it at most retail stores.

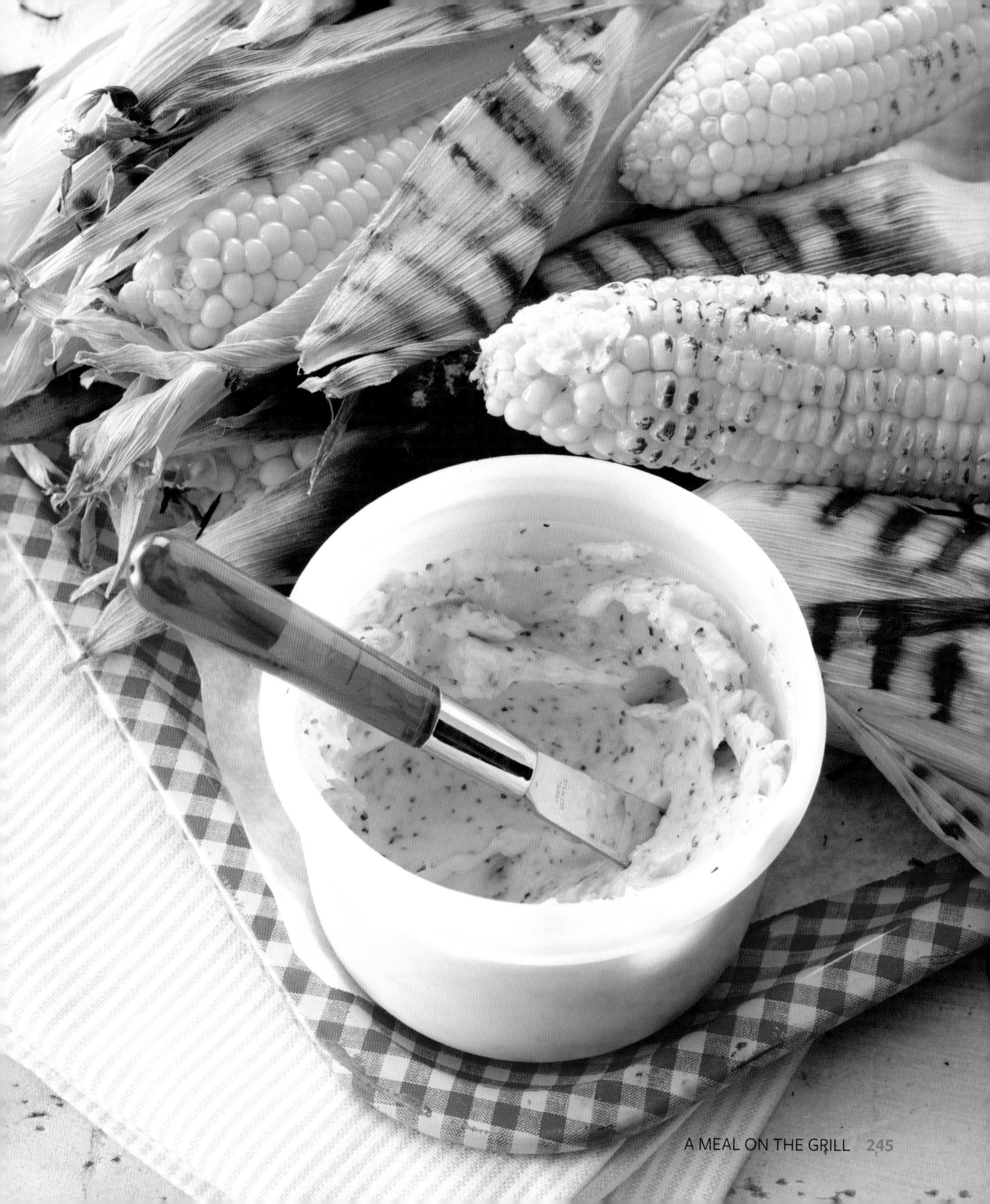

BARBECUED PICNIC CHICKEN

I like to serve this savory chicken at family picnics. Cooked on a covered grill, the poultry stays so tender and juicy. Everyone loves the zesty, slightly sweet homemade barbecue sauce—and it's so easy to make.
—Priscilla Weaver, Hagerstown, MD

Prep: 15 min. **Grill:** 45 min. **Makes:** 8 servings

2 garlic cloves, minced
2 teaspoons butter
1 cup ketchup
¼ cup packed brown sugar
¼ cup chili sauce
2 tablespoons Worcestershire sauce
1 tablespoon celery seed
1 tablespoon prepared mustard
½ teaspoon salt
2 dashes hot pepper sauce
2 broiler/fryer chickens (3½ to 4 pounds each), cut up

1. In a large saucepan, saute garlic in butter until tender. Add the next eight ingredients. Bring to a boil, stirring constantly. Remove from the heat; set sauce aside.

2. On a lightly greased grill rack, grill chicken, covered, over medium heat for 30 minutes, turning occasionally. Baste with sauce. Grill 15 minutes longer or until a thermometer reaches 170°, basting and turning several times.

HOW TO GRILL CHICKEN PARTS
(Pictured left, top to bottom)

- Stir the sauce constantly while bringing it to a boil; the sugar and the sauces can stick hard and fast to the bottom of pan otherwise.

- Oil the grill when hot. To prevent burns, use tongs to grip a paper towel or clean cloth dipped in oil and run it over the grill surface.

- Grill bone-in chicken pieces over medium heat. Never brush the barbecue sauce onto the chicken before you've turned it. Doing so risks transferring bacteria from the uncooked chicken to the cooked chicken.

- Sweet barbecue sauce will char if it's brushed onto the chicken too early in the cooking process; wait until the last 15 minutes of grilling. Keep a close eye on the chicken after adding the sauce.

✳

TEST KITCHEN TIP
This sauce is best when made a day or two in advance, giving the flavors time to come together. If you don't have chili sauce on hand, you can use ¼ cup extra ketchup or ¼ cup cocktail sauce.

ALL-AMERICAN HAMBURGERS

We do a lot of camping and outdoor cooking. Hamburgers are on our menu more than any other food.
—Diane Hixon, Niceville, FL

Start to Finish: 20 min. **Makes:** 4 servings

1 pound ground beef
2 tablespoons finely chopped onion
2 tablespoons chili sauce
2 teaspoons Worcestershire sauce
2 teaspoons prepared mustard
4 slices process American cheese or cheddar cheese, halved diagonally
2 slices Swiss cheese, halved diagonally
4 hamburger buns, split and toasted
   Lettuce leaves, sliced tomato and onion, cooked bacon strips, ketchup and mustard, optional

1. Combine the first five ingredients, mixing lightly but thoroughly. Shape into four patties. Grill burgers, covered, on a greased rack over medium direct heat until a thermometer reads 160° and juices run clear, about 6 minutes on each side.

2. During the last minute of cooking, top each patty with two triangles of American cheese and one triangle of Swiss cheese. Serve on buns; if desired, top with lettuce, tomato, onion, bacon, ketchup and/or mustard.

❋

TEST KITCHEN TIP
Avoid pressing down on burgers with a spatula—it'll squeeze out the juices, decreasing the overall flavor and increasing the chance of drying out the patties.

FOUR GREAT BURGER BOOSTERS

Top a burger, slather a sandwich or serve these combos on the side with grilled chicken or fish—or use as dips for fresh veggies!

- **Blue Cheese Bacon:** Combine ¼ cup mayonnaise, ¼ cup softened cream cheese, ⅓ cup crumbled blue cheese, ⅓ cup crumbled bacon and 2 tablespoons cider vinegar. Add salt and fresh cracked pepper to taste. Makes about 1 cup.

- **Chipotle BBQ:** Combine 1 cup mayonnaise, 3 tablespoons barbecue sauce, 1 tablespoon chopped chipotle peppers in adobo sauce and 2 tablespoons cider vinegar. Add salt and fresh cracked pepper to taste. Makes about 1¼ cups.

- **Spicy Thai:** Combine 1 cup mayonnaise, 1 tablespoon chili garlic paste, 1 tablespoon lime juice, 1 tablespoon lime peel, 2 tablespoons chopped cilantro and 1 sliced green onion. Add salt and fresh cracked pepper to taste. Makes about 1¼ cups.

- **Buffalo:** Combine 1 cup mayonnaise, ¼ cup softened cream cheese, ¼ cup crumbled blue cheese, 2 tablespoons hot sauce and 3 tablespoons minced celery. Add salt and fresh cracked pepper to taste. Makes about 1½ cups.

HOW TO MAKE
A TOPPER TIN

Use a muffin tin to double as a handy condiment caddy. Fill each compartment with your favorite toppings, and add mini serving spoons so guests can load up their burgers as they like.

BE A BURGER BOSS

MARINATED CHICKEN & ZUCCHINI KABOBS

These tasty and healthy kabobs are a favorite in our family, and they're so easy to make!
Change them up with turkey tenderloins and other veggies, like summer squash or sweet bell peppers.
—Tammy Slade, Stansbury Park, UT

Prep: 25 min. + marinating **Grill:** 10 min. **Makes:** 8 servings

¾ cup lemon-lime soda
½ cup reduced-sodium soy sauce
½ cup canola oil, divided
2 pounds boneless skinless chicken breasts or turkey breast tenderloins, cut into 1-inch cubes
3 medium zucchini, cut into 1-inch pieces
2 medium red onions, cut into 1-inch pieces
½ teaspoon salt
¼ teaspoon pepper

1. In a large resealable plastic bag, combine soda, soy sauce and ¼ cup oil. Add chicken; seal bag and turn to coat. Refrigerate 8 hours or overnight.

2. Drain chicken, discarding marinade. On eight metal or soaked wooden skewers, alternately thread chicken and vegetables. Brush vegetables with remaining oil; sprinkle with salt and pepper. On a greased grill, cook the kabobs, covered, over medium heat for 8-10 minutes or until chicken is no longer pink and vegetables are tender, turning occasionally.

✳
TEST KITCHEN TIP
Always throw out marinade if uncooked meat has been sitting in it. If the recipe calls for basting the meat with marinade at some point, be sure to reserve a small amount of marinade before adding the meat.

GRILLED MARINATED RIBEYES

These juicy steaks are a favorite meal of ours when we go camping. Let them sit overnight in their tangy, barbecue-inspired marinade and you've got a rich and hearty dinner ready to grill up the next day.
—Louise Graybiel, Toronto, ON

Prep: 10 min. + marinating **Grill:** 10 min. **Makes:** 4 servings

½ cup barbecue sauce
3 tablespoons Worcestershire sauce
3 tablespoons olive oil
2 tablespoons steak sauce
1 tablespoon red wine vinegar
1 tablespoon reduced-sodium soy sauce
2 teaspoons steak seasoning
1 teaspoon hot pepper sauce
1 garlic clove, minced
4 beef ribeye steaks (8 ounces each)

1. In a large resealable plastic bag, mix the first nine ingredients. Add steaks; seal bag and turn to coat. Refrigerate 4 hours or overnight.

2. Drain steaks, discarding marinade. Grill steaks, covered, over medium heat until meat reaches desired doneness (for medium-rare, a thermometer should read 135°; medium, 140°), 5-7 minutes per side.

To freeze: Freeze steaks with the marinade in a resealable plastic freezer bag. To use, thaw in the refrigerator overnight. Drain beef, discarding marinade. Grill as directed.

Note: This recipe was tested with McCormick's Montreal Steak Seasoning. Look for it in the spice aisle.

*

TEST KITCHEN TIP
To test steak for doneness, insert an instant-read thermometer horizontally from the side, making sure the reading is from the center of the meat.

WHY YOU'LL LOVE IT...
"Very flavorful. Wasn't sure about BBQ sauce and steak together but this marinade was amazing."
—DLSNOW52, TASTEOFHOME.COM

HOW TO GRILL STEAKS

(Pictured above, left to right)

- Whether you use the seasoning mixture in the recipe or simple salt and pepper, let the seasoned steaks stand for at least one hour. This helps to season deeper into the steak and tenderizes the meat.

- Removing excess moisture from the outside of the steaks before cooking is important—otherwise they won't get that nice, golden brown crust. Just before grilling, sprinkle on a bit of additional salt to replace some of what you dabbed off.

- Starting steaks over indirect heat helps them cook more evenly throughout. Move them to direct heat to crisp up and get a nice brown color just before serving.

- The steaks will cook more evenly if you flip them a few times. You won't get perfect crosshatch grill marks, but we think it's a worthwhile sacrifice to make.

- Let the steaks rest for at least one-quarter to one-third of the time it took to cook them. This helps redistribute the juices through the meat.

DESSERT
ON THE
GRILL!

GRILLED ANGEL FOOD CAKE WITH STRAWBERRIES

One night I goofed, accidentally using the balsamic butter I save for grilling chicken on my pound cake. What a delicious mistake! My entire family loved it.
—Tammy Hathaway, Freeman Township, ME

Start to Finish: 15 min. **Makes:** 8 servings

2 cups sliced fresh strawberries
2 teaspoons sugar
3 tablespoons butter, melted
2 tablespoons balsamic vinegar
8 slices angel food cake (about 1 ounce each)
Reduced-fat vanilla ice cream and blueberry syrup, optional

1. In a small bowl, toss strawberries with sugar. In another bowl, mix the butter and vinegar; brush over cut sides of cake.

2. On a greased rack, grill angel food cake, uncovered, over medium heat for 1-2 minutes on each side or until golden brown. Serve cake with the strawberries and, if desired, vanilla ice cream and blueberry syrup.

A MEAL THAT'S SLOW-COOKED

Imagine being able to come home to a meal that's already cooked, still warm and ready to eat. With a slow cooker, you can make this a reality! Try all of these set-and-forget recipes and you'll see why it's a go-to appliance for today's cooks.

SLOW COOKER SPINACH & ARTICHOKE DIP

With this creamy dip, I can get my daughters to eat spinach and artichokes.
We serve it with chips, toasted pita bread or fresh veggies.
—Jennifer Stowell, Montezuma, IA

Prep: 10 min. **Cook:** 2 hours **Makes:** 32 servings (¼ cup each)

- 2 cans (14 ounces each) water-packed artichoke hearts, drained and chopped
- 2 packages (10 ounces each) frozen chopped spinach, thawed and squeezed dry
- 1 jar (15 ounces) Alfredo sauce
- 1 package (8 ounces) cream cheese, cubed
- 2 cups shredded Italian cheese blend
- 1 cup shredded part-skim mozzarella cheese
- 1 cup shredded Parmesan cheese
- 1 cup 2% milk
- 2 garlic cloves, minced
  Assorted crackers and/or cucumber slices

In a greased 4-qt. slow cooker, combine the first nine ingredients. Cook mixture, covered, on low for 2-3 hours or until heated through. Serve with crackers and/or cucumber slices.

✳

TEST KITCHEN TIP
Wondering how to squeeze spinach dry? Use a colander! Put spinach in a colander to drain the moisture, then use clean hands to press the excess water from the spinach.

SLOW COOK WITH CONFIDENCE

- **Prep now, cook later:** In most cases, you can prepare and load ingredients into the slow cooker insert beforehand and store it in the refrigerator overnight. Keep in mind that an insert can crack if exposed to rapid temperature changes. Let the insert reach room temperature before placing it in the slow cooker.

- **Brown the meat:** Take a few extra minutes to brown meat in a skillet before placing it in the slow cooker. Doing so will add rich color and more flavor to the finished dish.

- **Don't lift that lid!** It's tempting to check on a meal's progress, but resist! Every time you open the lid, you'll have to add 15 to 30 minutes to the total cooking time.

- **Adjust cook time as needed:** Live at a high altitude? Slow cooking will take longer. Add about 30 minutes to each hour of cooking the recipe requires.

- **In a rush?** Cooking one hour on high is roughly equal to two hours on low, so adjust to your schedule.

SLOW COOKER HAM & EGGS

*This dish is great at any time of the year, but I love to make it for Easter morning.
I like to serve it with hash browns cooked up in the frying pan.*
—Andrea Schaak, Jordan, MN

Prep: 15 min. **Cook:** 3 hours **Makes:** 6 servings

6 large eggs
1 cup biscuit/baking mix
⅔ cup 2% milk
⅓ cup sour cream
2 tablespoons minced fresh parsley
2 garlic cloves, minced
½ teaspoon salt
½ teaspoon pepper
1 cup cubed fully cooked ham
1 cup shredded Swiss cheese
1 small onion, finely chopped
⅓ cup shredded Parmesan cheese

1. In a large bowl, whisk the first eight ingredients until blended; stir in the remaining ingredients. Pour into a greased 3- or 4-qt. slow cooker.

2. Cook, covered, on low 3-4 hours or until eggs are set. Cut into wedges.

SPLIT PEA SOUP WITH HAM & JALAPENO

*To me, this spicy pea soup is total comfort food. I cook it low and slow all day,
and it fills the house with a yummy aroma. It's so good with a nice, crispy baguette.*
—Chelsea Tichenor, Huntington Beach, CA

Prep: 15 min. **Cook:** 6 hours **Makes:** 6 servings (2¼ quarts)

2 smoked ham hocks
1 package (16 ounces) dried green split peas
4 medium carrots, cut into ½-inch slices
1 medium onion, chopped
1 jalapeno pepper, seeded and minced
3 garlic cloves, minced
8 cups water
1 teaspoon salt
1 teaspoon pepper

In a 4- or 5-qt. slow cooker, combine all ingredients. Cook, covered, on low until meat is tender, 6-8 hours. Remove meat from bones when cool enough to handle; cut ham into small pieces and return to slow cooker.

Note: Wear disposable gloves when cutting hot peppers; the oils can burn skin. Avoid touching your face.

HOW TO SEED A JALAPENO

Up to 80 percent of the capsaicin (the compound that gives peppers their heat) is in the seeds and membranes. To reduce the heat, cut the peppers in half and use a spoon to scrape out the seeds and membranes. If you like very spicy foods, add a few of the seeds back into the dish instead of merely discarding them.

BROCCOLI-CAULIFLOWER CHICKEN CASSEROLE

A chicken, broccoli and rice casserole is one of our favorite comfort foods. I make my easy variation in the slow cooker and prepare the rice separately. You can easily swap in whatever cheese you prefer. I sometimes use dairy-free cheese to create a more paleo-friendly dinner.
—Courtney Stultz, Weir, KS

Prep: 20 min. **Cook:** 4 hours **Makes:** 8 servings

2 pounds boneless skinless chicken breasts, cut into 1-inch pieces
1 small head cauliflower, chopped (about 4 cups)
1 bunch broccoli, chopped (about 4 cups)
½ pound medium fresh mushrooms, chopped
1 large onion, chopped
2 medium carrots, finely chopped
1 cup reduced-sodium chicken broth
4 ounces cream cheese, softened
2 tablespoons olive oil
2 teaspoons dried sage leaves
1 teaspoon salt
½ teaspoon pepper
1 cup shredded cheddar cheese
Hot cooked brown rice

In a 6-qt. slow cooker, combine the first six ingredients. In a small bowl, whisk broth, cream cheese, oil, sage, salt and pepper; pour over chicken mixture. Sprinkle with cheese. Cook, covered, on low 4-5 hours or until chicken and vegetables are tender. Serve with rice.

* Learn how to cook brown rice step by step by turning to page 215.

COMMON SLOW COOKER MISTAKES (AND HOW TO AVOID THEM)

Overcooking: Your family gave a slow-cooked dish low marks because of the mushy veggies, chalky meat or one-note flavors.

What to do instead: Use the slow cooker's Keep Warm setting if you need to leave something on longer than the recipe says. Or, choose a recipe that takes a full workday to cook, so it's ready when you are.

Using the wrong cuts of meat: You didn't have the cut of meat the recipe called for, so you swapped in something else and it didn't turn out great.

What to do instead: When slow cooking for an extended time, it's best to use well-marbled cuts. You can use less expensive meats, such as beef chuck roast, pork shoulder and chicken thighs.

Over- or under-filling the slow cooker: Either the contents almost bubbled over or you found your meal stuck to the bottom of the slow cooker.

What to do instead: Slow cookers operate best when filled halfway to three-quarters full. If cooking with more or less food, cooking times may need adjustment.

Chopping veggies too big or too small: That beef and veggie stew smelled so good. But some of the veggies were crunchy—hardly even crisp-tender—and others completely disappeared.

What to do instead: Cutting vegetables to the right size is key to achieving the best texture. They should all be about the same so they cook evenly.

POTLUCK BACON MAC & CHEESE

This wholesome mac and cheese is made with slow-cooked ease. Make it during the week or take it to your next potluck!
—Kelly Silvers, Edmond, OK

Prep: 30 min. **Cook:** 2 hours **Makes:** 8 servings

1   pound bacon strips, chopped
1   package (16 ounces) elbow macaroni
¼   cup all-purpose flour
2   teaspoons garlic powder
2   teaspoons onion powder
½   paprika, optional
2   cans (12 ounces each) evaporated milk
2   cups reduced-sodium chicken broth
8   ounces process cheese (Velveeta), cubed
2   cups shredded cheddar cheese

1. Fold two 18-in.-long pieces of foil into two 18x4-in. strips. Line perimeter of a 4-qt. slow cooker with foil strips; spray with cooking spray.

2. In a large skillet, cook bacon over medium heat until crisp, stirring occasionally. Remove bacon with a slotted spoon; drain on paper towels, reserving drippings. In the same skillet, heat 2 tablespoons bacon drippings over medium heat; cook the pasta in drippings 2 minutes or until edges turn translucent. Transfer to slow cooker.

3. In the same skillet, heat ¼ cup bacon drippings over medium heat. Add the flour, garlic powder, onion powder and, if desired, paprika. Cook and stir for 1-2 minutes or until flour begins to turn pale golden brown. Gradually whisk in milk and broth. Bring to a boil, stirring constantly; cook and stir 1-2 minutes or until thickened. Stir in cheeses; transfer to slow cooker. Stir in the pasta. Cook, covered, on low 2-3 hours or until pasta is tender. Top with bacon.

LINE THE CROCK FOR EASE OF USE

Some slow cooker recipes in this book call for a foil collar or sling. Here's why:

- A foil collar prevents rich, saucy dishes, such as this Potluck Bacon Mac & Cheese, from scorching near the slow cooker's heating element. To make a collar, fold two 18-in.-long pieces of foil into strips 4 in. wide. Line the crock's perimeter with the strips; spray with cooking spray.

- A sling (as seen above) helps you lift layered foods out of the crock without much fuss. To make, fold one or more pieces of heavy-duty foil into strips. Place on bottom and up sides of the slow cooker; coat with cooking spray.

BACON +
CHEESE +
PASTA = ♥

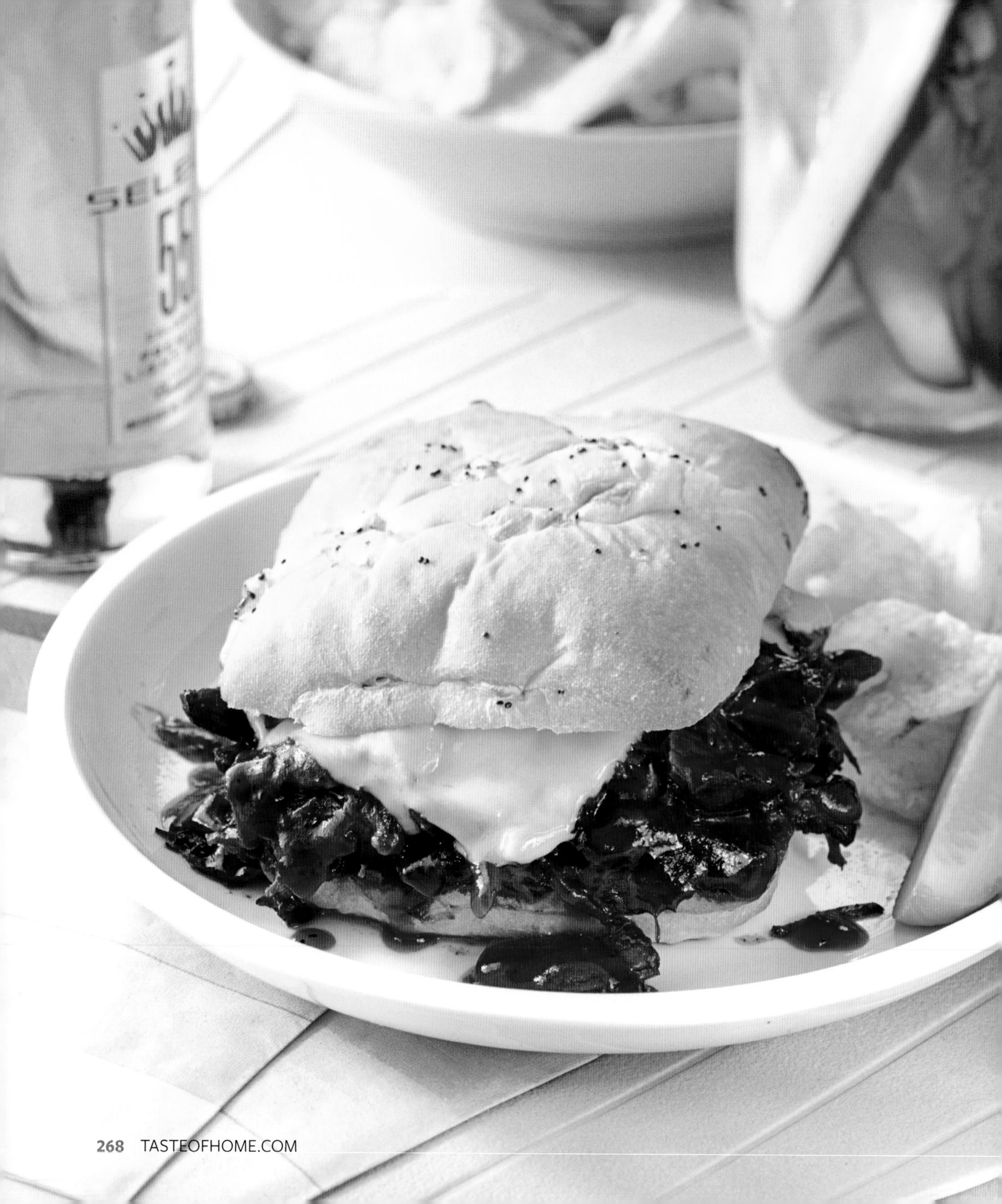

TEX-MEX SHREDDED BEEF SANDWICHES

Slow cooker meals, like this sandwich, are my favorite kind. I love having a hearty, satisfying feast when I come home!
—Kathy White, Henderson, NV

Prep: 5 min. **Cook:** 8 hours **Makes:** 8 servings

1 boneless beef chuck roast
   (3 pounds)
1 envelope chili seasoning
½ cup barbecue sauce
8 onion rolls, split
8 slices cheddar cheese

1. Cut roast in half; place in a 3-qt. slow cooker. Sprinkle with chili seasoning. Pour barbecue sauce over top. Cover and cook on low for 8-10 hours or until meat is tender.

2. Remove roast; cool slightly. Shred meat with two forks. Skim fat from cooking juices. Return meat to slow cooker; heat through. Using a slotted spoon, place ½ cup meat mixture on each roll bottom; top with cheese. Replace tops.

WHY YOU'LL LOVE IT...

"The whole family loved it. Doubled everything and gave some to another family. They requested the recipe. I made coleslaw to serve on the bun with it. Delicious!"

—2SOUTHERNSTARS, TASTEOFHOME.COM

SLOW COOKER PEACH CRUMBLE

I look forward to going on our beach vacation every year, but I don't always relish the time spent cooking for everybody. This slow cooker dessert (or breakfast!) gives me more time to lie in the sun and enjoy the waves. Melty ice cream is a must.
—Colleen Delawder, Herndon, VA

Prep: 20 min. **Cook:** 3 hours **Makes:** 8 servings

1 tablespoon butter, softened
6 large ripe peaches, peeled and sliced (about 6 cups)
2 tablespoons light brown sugar
1 tablespoon lemon juice
1 tablespoon vanilla extract
2 tablespoons coconut rum, optional

TOPPING
1 cup all-purpose flour
¾ cup packed light brown sugar
1½ teaspoons baking powder
1 teaspoon ground cinnamon
½ teaspoon baking soda
⅛ teaspoon salt
1 cup old-fashioned oats
6 tablespoons cold butter, cubed

1. Grease a 6-qt. oval slow cooker with 1 tablespoon softened butter. Toss peaches with brown sugar, lemon juice, vanilla and, if desired, rum; spread evenly in the slow cooker.

2. Whisk together first six topping ingredients; stir in oats. Cut in butter until crumbly; sprinkle over peaches. Cook, covered, on low until peaches are tender, 3-4 hours.

HOW TO PIT PEACHES

- Cut peach in half, cutting around the pit and using the peach's indentation as a guide.

- Twist the halves in opposite directions to separate. Using a sharp knife, loosen and remove the pit.

NO-BAKE CAKE!

MOLTEN MOCHA CAKE

*When I first made my slow cooker chocolate cake, my husband and daughter
loved it. My daughter says it's one of her most favorite desserts!*
—Aimee Fortney, Fairview, TN

Prep: 10 min. **Cook:** 2½ hours **Makes:** 4 servings

4 large eggs
1½ cups sugar
½ cup butter, melted
3 teaspoons vanilla extract
1 cup all-purpose flour
½ cup baking cocoa
1 tablespoon instant coffee granules
¼ teaspoon salt
   Fresh raspberries or sliced fresh
      strawberries and vanilla ice
      cream, optional

1. In a large bowl, beat eggs, sugar, butter and vanilla until blended. In another bowl, whisk flour, cocoa, coffee granules and salt; gradually beat into egg mixture.

2. Transfer to a greased 1½-qt. slow cooker. Cook, covered, on low for 2½-3 hours or until a toothpick comes out with moist crumbs. If desired, serve warm cake with berries and ice cream.

HOW TO MAKE ICE CREAM WITHOUT AN ICE CREAM MAKER

You'll need:
2 cups heavy whipping cream
2 cups half-and-half cream
1 cup sugar
2 teaspoons vanilla extract

- Freeze an empty freezer-safe shallow bowl or pan. We use a 13×9-inch pan, but anything stainless steel or Pyrex works well here. Avoid any material that might shatter.

- In a large bowl, stir all the ingredients until the sugar is dissolved. For the smoothest texture, make sure the sugar is completely dissolved before you freeze.

- Transfer the mixture into the cold pan and stick it back in the freezer for 20 to 30 minutes. Check the ice cream. Once the edges start to freeze, take the pan out of the freezer and beat the mixture using a hand mixer. Breaking up the ice cream helps make it smooth and creamy. You cannot beat it too much.

- Return the pan to the freezer. Every 30 minutes or so, take it out and beat the ice cream again. Repeat until it is firmly frozen; this usually takes four or five mixing sessions. Once it's frozen, the mixture should be smooth and creamy.

If at any time the ice cream becomes too hard, place it in the refrigerator until it becomes soft enough to beat, and then continue the process.

HOW DO I MAKE...

A MEAL THAT'S FREEZER-FRIENDLY

When you know you have a busy week coming up, let this chapter be your meal-planning guide. Since all these recipes are fit to be frozen, make them now to enjoy later (or right away, if you prefer)!

DELUXE HASH BROWN CASSEROLE

My son-in-law gave me the recipe for this hash brown casserole,
which my kids say is addictive. It's also an amazing make-ahead dish.
—Amy Oswalt, Burr, NE

Prep: 10 min. **Bake:** 50 min. **Makes:** 12 servings (⅔ cup each)

1½ cups sour cream onion dip
1 can (10¾ ounces) condensed cream of chicken soup, undiluted
1 envelope ranch salad dressing mix
1 teaspoon onion powder
1 teaspoon garlic powder
½ teaspoon pepper
1 package (30 ounces) frozen shredded hash brown potatoes, thawed
2 cups shredded cheddar cheese
½ cup crumbled cooked bacon

Preheat oven to 375°. In a large bowl, mix the first six ingredients; stir in potatoes, cheese and bacon. Transfer to a greased 13x9-in. baking dish. Bake 50-60 minutes or until golden brown.

To freeze: Cover and freeze unbaked casserole. To use, partially thaw in refrigerator overnight. Remove from refrigerator 30 minutes before baking. Preheat oven to 375°. Bake casserole as directed, increasing time to 1¼-1½ hours or until top is golden brown and a thermometer inserted in the center reads 165°.

FREEZER BASICS

Don't let the cold set in. It's essential to use the right containers, pack and store foods properly and choose freezer-friendly ingredients to maximize your deep-freeze potential.

- **Label everything:** Keep a marker and freezer labels handy, and jot the date and contents down on each container. Even if you can see what's inside, date the item so you won't have to guess how long it's been frozen.

- **Wrap it up:** Tightly wrap meats in plastic, then in heavy-duty foil or freezer paper, using freezer tape to seal if necessary. For other foods, use durable, leakproof containers or freezer bags. Press bags to remove all air before sealing. Store raw meats on the bottom shelf to minimize the potential for contamination.

- **Follow a plan:** First In, First Out (FIFO) is a simple practice that's used in grocery stores, restaurants and the food-service industry at large. It means you should use the oldest-dated foods first to avoid waste and keep grocery costs down.

- **Do monthly checkups:** Take a moment or two each month to get acquainted with the contents of your freezer. Reshuffle items, throw out or compost food that's been frozen for too long and defrost and use up forgotten treasures, like that stew your neighbor offered a month ago.

- **Make single servings:** A pound of bacon or an entire batch of cookie dough can be too much to thaw at once. Tightly seal smaller amounts separately, then store together in a large container.

- **Pack it flat:** Always allow hot food to cool to room temperature before freezing; once it's completely cool, freeze immediately. In many cases, it's helpful to freeze foods in a single layer (on a sheet pan, for example), and then stack them in a container or sturdy resealable freezer bag after they're frozen.

ON-THE-GO BREAKFAST MUFFINS

Family members frequently request that I make these muffins. I usually prepare them on Sunday night, so when we're running late on weekday mornings, the kids can grab these to eat on the bus.
—Irene Wayman, Grantsville, UT

Prep: 30 min. **Bake:** 15 min. **Makes:** 1½ dozen

1 pound bulk Italian sausage
7 large eggs, divided use
2 cups all-purpose flour
⅓ cup sugar
3 teaspoons baking powder
½ teaspoon salt
½ cup 2% milk
½ cup canola oil
1 cup shredded cheddar cheese, divided

1. Preheat oven to 400°. In a large nonstick skillet, cook sausage over medium heat 6-8 minutes or until no longer pink, breaking into crumbles. Remove with a slotted spoon; drain on paper towels. Wipe skillet clean.

2. In a small bowl, whisk five eggs. Pour into the same skillet; cook and stir over medium heat until thickened and no liquid egg remains. Remove from heat.

3. In a large bowl, whisk flour, sugar, baking powder and salt. In another bowl, whisk remaining eggs, milk and oil until blended. Add to flour mixture; stir just until moistened. Fold in ⅔ cup cheese, sausage and scrambled eggs.

4. Fill greased or paper-lined muffin cups three-fourths full. Sprinkle tops with remaining cheese. Bake muffins for 12-15 minutes or until a toothpick inserted in center comes out clean. Cool 5 minutes before removing from pans to wire racks. Serve warm.

To freeze: Freeze cooled muffins in resealable plastic freezer bags. To use, microwave each muffin on high for 45-60 seconds or until heated through.

WHY YOU'LL LOVE IT...
"These muffins are fantastic! I substituted a pound of bacon and added a tablespoon of dried chives. They were super easy to make and had just the right balance of sweet and savory."
—CAROLYNCONNER, TASTEOFHOME.COM

CHICKEN BUTTERNUT CHILI

At our house, we love a comforting, hearty, tomato-based chili with bold flavors! This unique chili is loaded with veggies. It can also be prepared in the slow cooker; simply add the ingredients and cook on high for about 4 hours.
—Courtney Stultz, Weir, KS

Prep: 20 min. **Cook:** 35 min. **Makes:** 4 servings

1 tablespoon canola oil
2 medium carrots, chopped
2 celery ribs, chopped
1 medium onion, chopped
2 cups cubed peeled butternut squash
1 medium tomato, chopped
2 tablespoons tomato paste
1 envelope reduced-sodium chili seasoning mix
2 cups chicken stock
1 cup cubed cooked chicken breast
Chopped fresh cilantro

1. In a large saucepan, heat oil over medium heat; saute carrots, celery and onion until tender, 6-8 minutes.

2. Stir in squash, tomato, tomato paste, seasoning mix and stock; bring to a boil. Reduce heat; simmer, covered, until squash is tender, 20-25 minutes. Stir in chicken; heat through. Sprinkle with cilantro.

To freeze: Freeze cooled chili in freezer containers. To use, partially thaw in refrigerator overnight. Heat through in a saucepan, stirring occasionally.

HOW TO STAY ORGANIZED

- Divide the freezer into zones, with areas for veggies, breads, meats, etc., so you always know where to look.

- Label strategically with masking tape and a permanent marker. Include the date the food was prepared and when it went in so you know if it's getting old. Use different-colored markers for different types of food—poultry, seafood, sauces—so you can find what you want at a glance.

- Combine similar items. If you have four packages of frozen berries, put them all into one larger plastic bag or a plastic basket, then label the container. Like berries, nuts will stay fresh longer in the freezer. Store bags of various kinds of nuts in one large freezer bag.

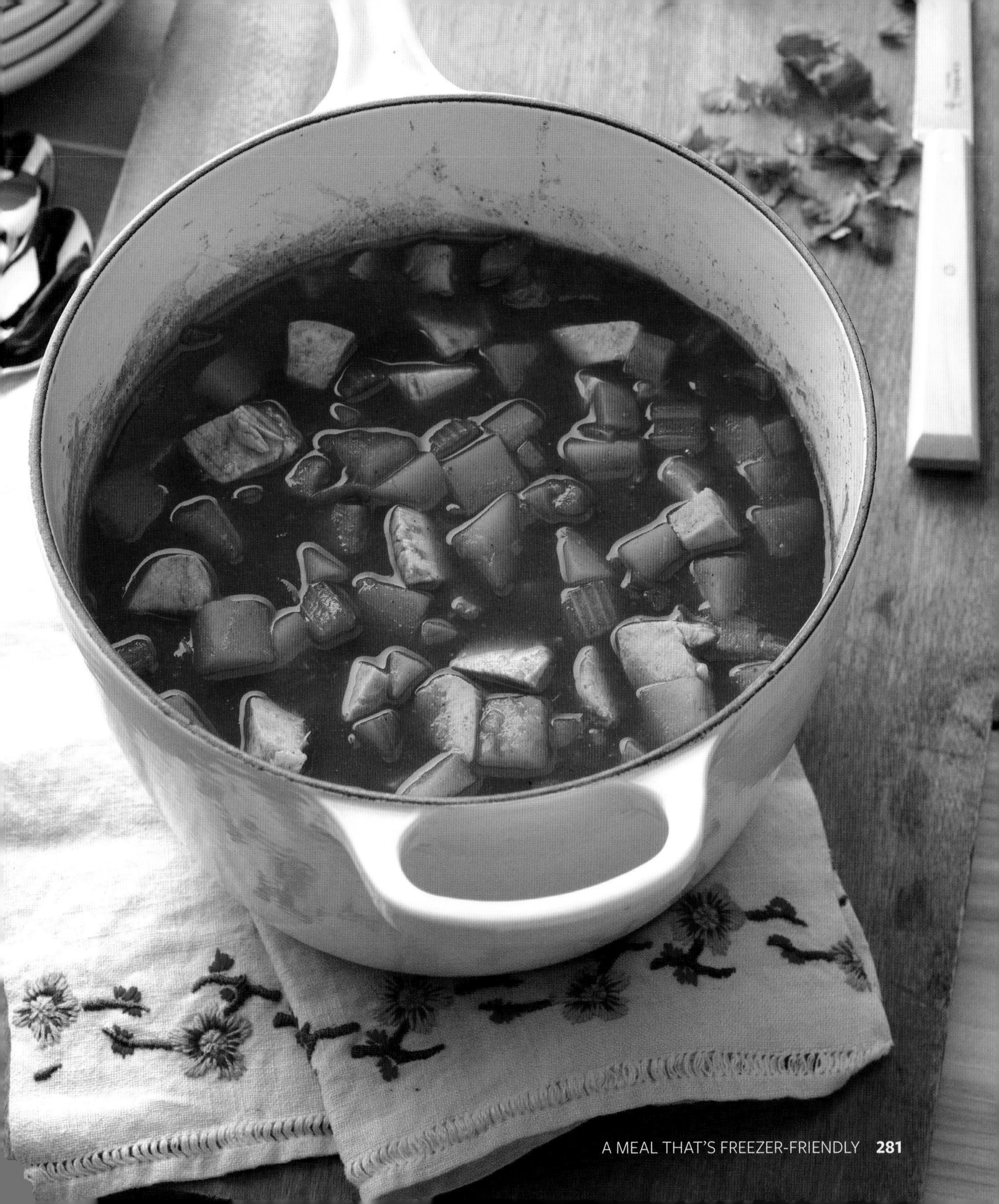

BETTER THAN TAKEOUT!

SLOW COOKER SWEET-AND-SOUR PORK

*Chinese food is a big temptation for us, so I lightened up a favorite
takeout dish. As the pork cooks, the aroma is beyond mouthwatering.*
—Elyse Ellis, Layton, UT

Prep: 15 min. **Cook:** 6¼ hours **Makes:** 4 servings

½ cup sugar
½ cup packed brown sugar
½ cup chicken broth
⅓ cup white vinegar
3 tablespoons lemon juice
3 tablespoons reduced-sodium soy sauce
3 tablespoons tomato paste
½ teaspoon garlic powder
¼ teaspoon ground ginger
¼ teaspoon pepper
1½ pounds boneless pork loin chops, cut into 1-inch cubes
1 large onion, cut into 1-inch pieces
1 large green pepper, cut into 1-inch pieces
1 can (8 ounces) pineapple chunks, drained

ADDITIONAL INGREDIENTS
3 tablespoons cornstarch
⅓ cup chicken broth
Hot cooked rice

1. In a 3- or 4-qt. slow cooker, mix the first 10 ingredients. Stir in pork, onion, green pepper and pineapple. Cook, covered, on low 6-8 hours or until pork is tender.

2. In a small bowl, mix cornstarch and broth until smooth; gradually stir into cooking juices. Cook, covered, on low 15-20 minutes longer or until sauce is thickened. Serve with rice.

To freeze: In a large resealable plastic freezer bag, combine the first 10 ingredients. Add pork, onion, green pepper and pineapple; seal bag, turn to coat, then freeze. To use, place filled freezer bag in refrigerator for 48 hours or until its contents are completely thawed. Cook as directed.

HOW TO THAW SAFELY

• Defrosting in the refrigerator is safe and fuss-free, but it's the slowest method, so plan ahead. Smaller items, like a pound of ground beef, defrost overnight. Many items take 1 or 2 days. For small beef and pork roasts, allow 3 to 5 hours per pound of meat; for larger cuts, allow 5 to 7 hours. A whole turkey will take 24 hours for every 4 to 5 pounds of weight.

• Defrosting with cold water is faster than the refrigerator but requires more attention. Place the food in a watertight plastic storage bag; place bag in cold water. Change the water every 30 minutes until food is thawed.

• Defrosting in the microwave is suitable for last-minute thawing of small items. Unwrap the food and place it in a microwave-safe dish. Cook the food immediately after defrosting.

MAKE-AHEAD SAUSAGE PINWHEELS

Besides being easy to make, these roll-ups can be done way ahead and kept in the freezer. All you have to do is pop them into a hot oven!
—Cindy Nerat, Menominee, MI

Prep: 1 hour + freezing **Bake:** 15 min. **Makes:** about 6½ dozen

- 1 **pound bulk regular or spicy pork sausage**
- ½ **cup diced sweet red pepper**
- 1 **green onion, chopped**
- 1 **package (8 ounces) cream cheese, cubed**
- 2 **tubes (8 ounces each) refrigerated crescent rolls**

1. Preheat oven to 350°. In a large skillet, cook and crumble sausage over medium-high heat until no longer pink, 5-7 minutes; drain. Add pepper and green onion; cook and stir 2 minutes. Transfer to a bowl; cool 10 minutes. Stir in the cream cheese until blended; cool mixture completely.

2. Unroll one can of crescent dough and separate into four rectangles; pinch the perforations to seal. Press each rectangle to 6x4½ in.; spread each with ⅓ cup filling to within ¼ in. of edges. Roll up jelly-roll style, starting with a short side; pinch seam to seal. Roll gently to make logs smooth. Place on a waxed paper-lined baking sheet, seam side down. Repeat with remaining crescent dough. Freeze, covered, until firm, about 1 hour.

3. Cut each log into 10 slices. Bake on parchment paper-lined baking sheets until golden brown, 15-18 minutes. Serve warm.

To freeze: Freeze pinwheels in freezer containers, separating layers with waxed paper. To use, bake the frozen pinwheels as directed, increasing time by 3-5 minutes.

*

TEST KITCHEN TIP
Peppers are freshest in mid-summer. Look for ones that have firm, smooth glossy skin; avoid peppers that are shriveled or have soft spots. Refrigerate, unwashed, for up to 5 days.

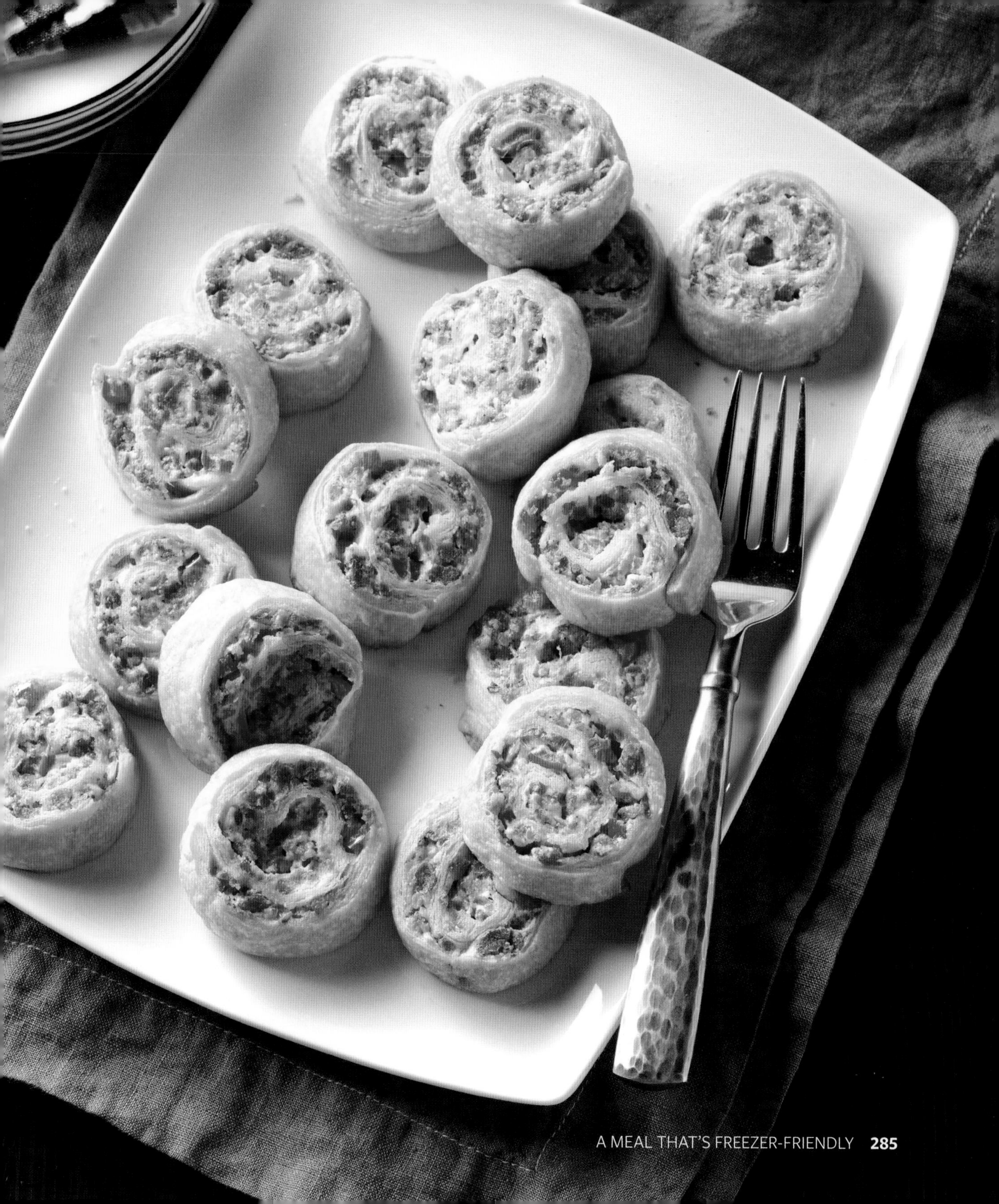

CHICKEN TACOS WITH AVOCADO SALSA

These zesty tacos suit everyone. For extra toppings, add cilantro, red onion, jalapeno, black olives and lettuce.
—Christine Schenher, Exeter, CA

Start to Finish: 30 min. **Makes:** 4 servings

1 pound boneless skinless chicken breasts, cut into ½-inch strips
⅓ cup water
1 teaspoon sugar
1 tablespoon chili powder
1 teaspoon onion powder
1 teaspoon dried oregano
1 teaspoon ground cumin
1 teaspoon paprika
½ teaspoon salt
½ teaspoon garlic powder
1 medium ripe avocado, peeled and cubed
1 cup fresh or frozen corn, thawed
1 cup cherry tomatoes, quartered
2 teaspoons lime juice
8 taco shells, warmed

1. Place a large nonstick skillet coated with cooking spray over medium-high heat. Brown chicken. Add water, sugar and seasonings. Cook 4-5 minutes or until chicken is no longer pink, stirring occasionally.

2. Meanwhile, in a small bowl, gently mix avocado, corn, tomatoes and lime juice. Spoon chicken mixture into taco shells; top with avocado salsa.

To freeze: Freeze cooled chicken mixture in freezer containers. To use, partially thaw in refrigerator overnight. Heat through in a saucepan, stirring occasionally and adding a little water if necessary.

* After digging into these tacos, cool off with a refreshing drink. Flip to page 14 to find some sweet sips.

USE 'EM OR LOSE 'EM

Even frozen foods don't last forever; the quality is bound to diminish with time. Use this list for easy reference.

- **Baked cookies:** 8-12 months
- **Baked pie:** 1-2 months
- **Baked quick bread:** 2-3 months
- **Butter:** 6-9 months
- **Casseroles:** 2-3 months
- **Cheese, hard or soft:** 6 months
- **Cheesecake:** 2-3 months
- **Cooked chicken pieces:** 4 months
- **Cooked fish:** 4-6 months
- **Cooked shrimp:** 3 months
- **Frozen veggies:** 8 months
- **Ground beef:** 4 months
- **Ice cream:** 2 months
- **Soups and stews:** 2-3 months
- **Uncooked bacon:** 1 month
- **Uncooked chicken pieces:** 9 months
- **Uncooked pork chops:** 4-6 months
- **Uncooked steak:** 6-12 months
- **Whole chicken or turkey:** 12 months
- **Yeast bread or rolls:** 3-6 months

ITALIAN SAUSAGE RIGATONI BAKE

Here's a dish that combines all of our favorite Italian flavors. The fresh mozzarella really sets it apart!
—Blair Lonergan, Rochelle, VA

Prep: 30 min. **Bake:** 25 min. **Makes:** 2 casseroles (4 servings each)

1 package (16 ounces) rigatoni
1 pound bulk Italian sausage
½ pound sliced fresh mushrooms
1 medium sweet red pepper, chopped
5 cups marinara sauce
¼ cup grated Parmesan cheese
2 tablespoons half-and-half cream
1 pound sliced part-skim mozzarella cheese

1. Preheat oven to 375°. Cook rigatoni according to package directions; drain.

2. In a large skillet, cook sausage, mushrooms and pepper over medium-high heat 8-10 minutes or until sausage is no longer pink and vegetables are tender, breaking up the sausage into crumbles; drain. Stir in marinara sauce, Parmesan cheese and cream. Add rigatoni and toss to coat.

3. In each of two greased 8-in. square baking dishes, layer one-fourth of the rigatoni mixture and one-fourth of the mozzarella cheese. Repeat layers. Bake uncovered for 25-35 minutes or until heated through and cheese is melted. (Cover loosely with foil if tops brown too quickly.)

To freeze: Cool unbaked casseroles; cover and freeze. To use, partially thaw in refrigerator overnight. Remove from refrigerator 30 minutes before baking. Preheat oven to 375°. Bake casseroles as directed, increasing the time as necessary to heat through and for a thermometer inserted in center to read 165°.

WHY YOU'LL LOVE IT...

"This was excellent, and the leftovers were just as tasty! I ended up using shredded mozzarella since I had it on hand and it was delicious."

—NAN MOCK, TASTEOFHOME.COM

YOU HAVE TO TRY THIS!

SIMPLE CREAMY CHICKEN ENCHILADAS

This is one of the first recipes I created and cooked for my husband right after we got married. He was so impressed!
—Melissa Rogers, Tuscaloosa, AL

Prep: 30 min. **Bake:** 30 min. **Makes:** 2 casseroles (5 servings each)

2 cans (14½ ounces each) diced tomatoes with mild green chilies, undrained

2 cans (10½ ounces each) condensed cream of chicken soup, undiluted

1 can (10¾ ounces) condensed cheddar cheese soup, undiluted

¼ cup 2% milk

1 tablespoon ground cumin

1 tablespoon chili powder

2 teaspoons garlic powder

2 teaspoons dried oregano

5 cups shredded rotisserie chicken

1 package (8 ounces) cream cheese, cubed and softened

20 flour tortillas (8 inches), warmed

4 cups shredded Mexican cheese blend

1. Preheat oven to 350°. For sauce, mix first eight ingredients. For filling, in a large bowl, mix chicken and cream cheese until blended; stir in 3½ cups of sauce.

2. Spread ¼ cup sauce into each of two greased 13x9-in. baking dishes. Place ⅓ cup filling down the center of each tortilla; roll up and place seam side down in baking dishes. Pour remaining sauce over tops; sprinkle with cheese.

3. Bake, uncovered, 30-35 minutes or until heated through and the cheese is melted.

To freeze: Cover and freeze unbaked casseroles for up to 3 months. To use, partially thaw in refrigerator overnight. Remove from refrigerator 30 minutes before baking. Preheat oven to 350°. Cover casserole with greased foil; bake 45 minutes or until heated through and a thermometer inserted in the center reads 165°. Uncover; bake 5-10 more minutes or until cheese is melted.

FREEZE IT BETTER!

- Use a thermometer to monitor your freezer. For optimum quality, it should be 0°.

- Cool food quickly and evenly before freezing. Transfer hot foods to a large shallow pan or several small, shallow containers, or place the hot pan into a bowl of ice water. Stir frequently to help the food cool faster.

- Freeze a small amount first if you're not sure how something will freeze. After it's thawed and reheated (if necessary), decide if the quality is up to your standards.

- Season sparingly before freezing, and add more later if necessary. Spices tend to change somewhat during freezer storage.

- Leave some space around each package so air can circulate.

- Manage the quantities so whatever is placed in the freezer is frozen solid within 24 hours. Adding a lot of food at once will increase freezing time.

- Store nuts, flour and juice in and/or near the door; save the colder parts of the freezer for other foods.

ICE CREAM SANDWICH COOKIES

This treat is snack heaven: ice cream, delicious oatmeal cookies and a touch of chocolate.
Swap out the vanilla for your favorite flavor, such as chocolate, caramel, mint chocolate chip or cherry.
—Jacyn Siebert, San Francisco, CA

Prep: 40 min. + freezing **Bake:** 15 min./batch + cooling **Makes:** 7 servings

½ cup butter, softened
¾ cup packed brown sugar
¼ cup sugar
1 large egg
½ teaspoon vanilla extract
¾ cup all-purpose flour
½ teaspoon baking soda
½ teaspoon ground cinnamon
¼ teaspoon baking powder
¼ teaspoon salt
1½ cups quick-cooking oats
¼ cup chopped raisins, optional

ASSEMBLY

3 cups vanilla ice cream
1 bottle (7¼ ounces) chocolate hard-shell ice cream topping

* Want to go the homemade ice cream route? Check out page 273.

1. Preheat oven to 350°. In a large bowl, cream butter and sugars until light and fluffy. Beat in egg and vanilla. In another bowl, whisk flour, baking soda, cinnamon, baking powder and salt; gradually beat into creamed mixture. Stir in oats and, if desired, raisins.

2. Shape dough into fourteen 1¼-in. balls; place 2½ in. apart on ungreased baking sheets. Bake until golden brown, 11-13 minutes. Cool on pans 3 minutes. Remove cookies to wire racks to cool completely.

3. To assemble ice cream sandwiches, place ⅓ cup ice cream on bottom of a cookie. Top with a second cookie, pressing gently to flatten ice cream. Place on a baking sheet; freeze until firm. Repeat with remaining cookies and ice cream.

4. Remove ice cream sandwiches from the freezer. Working over a small bowl, drizzle the chocolate topping over half of each sandwich, allowing excess to drip off.

5. Place on a waxed paper-lined baking sheet; freeze until serving. Wrap the sandwiches individually in plastic for longer storage.

HOW TO MAKE ICE CREAM SANDWICHES
(Pictured bottom right, left to right)

- The ice cream should be just soft enough to scoop easily but not starting to melt. Work quickly; when you've gotten two or three sandwiches made, pop them in the freezer before assembling the rest.

- Press down gently to force the ice cream just a little bit past the edge of the cookie. Don't overfill the sandwich; keep in mind how wide you can open your mouth!

- For a chocolate coating, drizzle the sandwich with hard-shell topping. You can also skip the coating and roll the edge of the sandwiches in mini chocolate chips, sprinkles or chopped nuts.

- If you're not serving immediately, wrap the sandwiches individually in plastic. Prepared sandwich cookies can be frozen for up to three months, but we bet these won't last that long!

HOW DO I MAKE...

A SPECIAL MEAL

It's time for the big show: We're going to show you how to successfully prepare a holiday meal (or perhaps just a classy dinner to impress). Master the beloved traditional dishes that are must-haves at special occasions.

MAPLE-WALNUT SWEET POTATOES

Sweet potatoes with dried cherries and walnuts make this side so delectable!
—Sarah Herse, Brooklyn, NY

Prep: 15 min. **Cook:** 5 hours **Makes:** 12 servings (¾ cup each)

4 pounds sweet potatoes (about 8 medium)
¾ cup coarsely chopped walnuts, divided
½ cup packed light brown sugar
½ cup dried cherries, coarsely chopped
½ cup maple syrup
¼ cup apple cider or juice
¼ teaspoon salt

1. Peel and cut sweet potatoes lengthwise in half; cut crosswise into ½-in. slices. Place in a 5-qt. slow cooker. Add ½ cup of walnuts, brown sugar, cherries, syrup, cider and salt; toss to combine.

2. Cook, covered, on low 5-6 hours or until potatoes are tender. Sprinkle with remaining walnuts.

✳

TEST KITCHEN TIP
Once sweet potatoes are cooked, you can store them in the refrigerator for up to 1 week.

SIMPLE VEGETARIAN SLOW-COOKED BEANS

When I have a hungry family to feed—which is often!—these tasty beans with spinach, tomatoes and carrots are a menu go-to.
—Jennifer Reid, Farmington, ME

Prep: 15 min. **Cook:** 4 hours **Makes:** 8 servings

4 cans (15½ ounces each) great northern beans, rinsed and drained
4 medium carrots, finely chopped (about 2 cups)
1 cup vegetable stock
6 garlic cloves, minced
2 teaspoons ground cumin
¾ teaspoon salt
⅛ teaspoon chili powder
4 cups fresh baby spinach, coarsely chopped
1 cup oil-packed sun-dried tomatoes, patted dry and chopped
⅓ cup minced fresh cilantro
⅓ cup minced fresh parsley

In a 3-qt. slow cooker, combine the first seven ingredients. Cook, covered, on low for 4-5 hours or until carrots are tender, adding spinach and tomatoes during the last 10 minutes of cooking. Stir in cilantro and parsley.

✳

TEST KITCHEN TIP
Recipes like this one advise rinsing and draining canned beans in part because salt is added during the canning process. Rinsing removes that unwanted sodium.

SIMPLY
SLOW
COOKED

MICHIGAN CHERRY SALAD

This recipe conjures what I love about my home state: apple picking with my children, buying greens at the farmers market and the taste of fresh cherries.
—Jennifer Gilbert, Brighton, MI

Start to Finish: 15 min. **Makes:** 8 servings

7 ounces fresh baby spinach (about 9 cups)
3 ounces spring mix salad greens (about 5 cups)
1 large apple, chopped
½ cup coarsely chopped pecans, toasted
½ cup dried cherries
¼ cup crumbled Gorgonzola cheese

DRESSING

¼ cup fresh raspberries
¼ cup red wine vinegar
3 tablespoons cider vinegar
3 tablespoons cherry preserves
1 tablespoon sugar
2 tablespoons olive oil

1. In a large bowl, combine the first six ingredients.

2. Place the raspberries, vinegars, preserves and sugar in a blender. While processing, gradually add oil in a steady stream. Drizzle over salad; toss to coat.

Note: To toast nuts, bake in a shallow pan in a 350° oven for 5-10 minutes or cook in a skillet over low heat until lightly browned, stirring occasionally.

✳

TEST KITCHEN TIP
Thanks to the high fat content of nuts, they can be toasted in a dry skillet. So, rather than adding oil, simply heat the skillet until hot, then pour the nuts in and spread them out in a single layer. Cook for 3-5 minutes, stirring often to keep them from turning too brown.

WHY YOU'LL LOVE IT...

"I thought this was delicious. I normally make all of my salad dressings and have never made one with berries in it. Brilliant idea. My dinner guests loved it and I am planning on making it for Thanksgiving."

—RLCURRY1, TASTEOFHOME.COM

NANNY'S PARMESAN MASHED POTATOES

My grandsons rave over these creamy potatoes loaded with Parmesan. That's all the endorsement I need. Sometimes I use golden or red potatoes, leaving the skins on.
—Kallee Krong-Mccreery, Escondido, CA

Prep: 20 min. **Cook:** 20 min. **Makes:** 12 servings (¾ cup each)

- 5 pounds potatoes, peeled and cut into 1-inch pieces
- ¾ cup butter, softened
- ¾ cup sour cream
- ½ cup grated Parmesan cheese
- 1¼ teaspoons garlic salt
- 1 teaspoon salt
- ½ teaspoon pepper
- ¾ to 1 cup 2% milk, warmed
- 2 tablespoons minced fresh parsley

1. Place potatoes in a 6-qt. stockpot; add water to cover. Bring to a boil. Reduce the heat; cook, uncovered, 10-15 minutes or until tender. Drain potatoes; return to pot and stir over low heat 1 minute to dry.

2. Coarsely mash potatoes, gradually adding butter, sour cream, cheese, seasonings and enough milk to reach desired consistency. Stir in parsley.

PICKING POTATOES

Whether you're mashing, baking or frying, the type of potato you use will influence the outcome. Potatoes fall into one of three categories: starchy, waxy and all-purpose. For the tastiest results, choose the type that best fits your cooking method.

Russet: High starch, low moisture

- Thicker skin and fluffy flesh
- Good for baking, boiling, mashing and frying
- Flesh breaks down when cooked, so best used for recipes with a smooth texture

Yukon Gold: Medium starch, high moisture

- Thinner skin and firm, waxy flesh
- Good for boiling, baking, mashing, frying, roasting and grilling
- Stands up well to most cooking applications, so a good choice for many dishes

Red/New: Low starch, high moisture

- Thinner skin and creamy, waxy flesh
- Good for roasting, boiling, salads, casseroles and soups
- Firm flesh holds up well, so best used in dishes where the potato needs to maintain its shape

TIPS FOR MAKING MASHED POTATOES

(Pictured above, left to right)

- Cut all the potatoes to roughly the same size. If the size varies too much, the potatoes will cook unevenly.

- Cover the cubed potatoes completely with water. Make sure they're covered or they may dry out. Then boil gently.

- While most cooks mash their potatoes with milk, others prefer to use cream. Do whatever you prefer!

- Cooking for someone who's dairy-free? You can mash the potatoes with unsweetened almond or soy milk, warmed chicken broth or even some of the starchy cooking water.

BASIL CORN & TOMATO BAKE

When Jersey sweet corn isn't in season, I use frozen. My cheesy corn bake can be served for breakfast, lunch or dinner.
—Erin Chilcoat, Central Islip, NY

Prep: 30 min. **Bake:** 45 min. + standing **Makes:** 10 servings

2 teaspoons olive oil
1 medium onion, chopped
2 large eggs
1 can (10¾ ounces) reduced-fat reduced-sodium condensed cream of celery soup, undiluted
4 cups fresh or frozen corn
1 small zucchini, chopped
1 medium tomato, seeded and chopped
¾ cup soft whole wheat bread crumbs
⅓ cup minced fresh basil
½ teaspoon salt
½ cup shredded part-skim mozzarella cheese
Additional minced fresh basil, optional

1. Preheat oven to 350°. In a small skillet, heat oil over medium heat. Add onion; cook and stir until tender. In a large bowl, whisk eggs and condensed soup until blended. Stir in vegetables, bread crumbs, basil, salt and onion. Transfer mixture to an 11x7-in. baking dish coated with cooking spray.

2. Bake, uncovered, 40-45 minutes or until bubbly. Sprinkle with the cheese. Bake for 5-10 minutes longer or until cheese is melted. Let stand 10 minutes before serving. If desired, sprinkle with additional basil.

Note: To make soft bread crumbs, tear bread into pieces and place in a food processor or blender. Cover and pulse until crumbs form. One slice of bread yields ½-¾ cup crumbs.

WHY YOU'LL LOVE IT...

"This is a great side dish to serve with almost any meal. I substituted the cream of celery soup for cream of mushroom and it turned out great. I also added a dash of cayenne pepper for a little heat."

—CRUMEJ, TASTEOFHOME.COM

SLOW COOKER TURKEY BREAST WITH GRAVY

This quick-prep recipe lets you feast on turkey at any time of year.
We save the rich broth for gravy, noodles and soup.
—Joyce Hough, Annapolis, MD

Prep: 25 min. **Cook:** 5 hours + standing **Makes:** 12 servings

2 teaspoons dried parsley flakes
1 teaspoon salt
1 teaspoon poultry seasoning
½ teaspoon paprika
½ teaspoon pepper
2 medium onions, chopped
3 medium carrots, cut into ½-inch slices
3 celery ribs, coarsely chopped
1 bone-in turkey breast (6 to 7 pounds), skin removed
¼ cup all-purpose flour
½ cup water

1. Mix first five ingredients in a small bowl. Place vegetables in a 6- or 7-qt. slow cooker; top with turkey. Rub turkey with seasoning mixture.

2. Cook, covered, on low until a thermometer inserted in the turkey reads at least 170°, 5-6 hours. Remove from slow cooker; let stand, covered, 15 minutes before slicing.

3. Meanwhile, strain the cooking juices into a small saucepan. Mix flour and water until smooth; stir into cooking juices. Bring to a boil; cook and stir until thickened, 1-2 minutes. Serve with the turkey.

HOW TO CARVE A SEMI-BONELESS HAM

(Pictured above, left to right)

When setting up your slicing station, don't crowd into a too-small area. We suggest a large cutting board at a normal working height, with space to shift your slices and plenty of elbow room.

- A semi-boneless ham has one bone running through it. Arrange the ham on the board with the pre-cut side down and the bone perpendicular to the board. Pierce a carving fork into the top corner of the meat—out of the way of the knife but deep enough to hold the meat stable. Use a sharp knife with a long, thin blade to carve along the bone.

- Carve the boneless section into vertical slices. Set the slices on a serving plate and tent with foil.

- Place the remaining section of meat on the board. Insert the carving fork next to the bone. Make horizontal cuts through the meat up to the bone.

- Slice vertically along the bone. This will cut off the horizontal slices, which will fall onto the board. Transfer them to the serving plate.

SPICE-RUBBED HAM

Now this is a ham—it's sweet and smoky, with just the right amount of cloves and ginger.
—Sharon Tipton, Winter Garden, FL

Prep: 15 min. **Bake:** 3¼ hours + standing **Makes:** 24 servings

1 fully cooked semi-boneless ham
  (8 to 10 pounds)
½ cup spicy brown mustard
¼ cup packed brown sugar
¼ teaspoon ground ginger
¼ teaspoon ground cinnamon
  Whole cloves

1. Place ham on a rack in a shallow roasting pan. Score the surface of the ham, making diamond shapes ½ in. deep. Combine the mustard, brown sugar, ginger and cinnamon; rub over surface of the ham. Insert a clove in the center of each diamond.

2. Bake ham, uncovered, at 325° for 1½ hours. Cover and bake 1¾-2 hours longer or until a thermometer reads 140°. Discard cloves. Let stand for 10 minutes before slicing.

✱

TEST KITCHEN TIP
Is scoring the ham worthwhile?
It is! Scoring opens up the fatty outer layer of the ham, allowing the glaze to penetrate the meat.

CARAMEL FLUFF & TOFFEE TRIFLE

The best part of this stunning dessert is you need just five ingredients to put it together.
—Daniel Anderson, Kenosha, WI

Prep: 15 min. + chilling **Makes:** 12 servings

2 cups heavy whipping cream
¾ cup packed brown sugar
1 teaspoon vanilla extract
1 prepared angel food cake (8 to 10 ounces), cut into 1-inch cubes
1 cup milk chocolate English toffee bits

1. In a large bowl, beat cream, brown sugar and vanilla just until blended. Refrigerate, covered, 20 minutes. Beat until stiff peaks form.

2. In a 4-qt. glass bowl, layer one-third of each of the following: cake cubes, whipped cream and toffee bits. Repeat layers twice. Refrigerate until serving.

✳ TEST KITCHEN TIP
There's a difference between soft peaks and stiff peaks. For stiff peaks, the whipping cream should stand up straight when you lift the beater from the mixture after beating.

EASY PUMPKIN PIE

Pumpkin pie is not difficult to make, and this recipe has wonderful flavor. It's sure to be a hit at your holiday meal.
—Marty Rummel, Trout Lake, WA

Prep: 10 min. **Bake:** 50 min. + cooling **Makes:** 8 servings

3 large eggs
1 cup canned pumpkin
1 cup evaporated milk
½ cup sugar
¼ cup maple syrup
1 teaspoon ground cinnamon
½ teaspoon salt
½ teaspoon ground nutmeg
½ teaspoon maple flavoring
½ teaspoon vanilla extract
1 frozen deep-dish pie shell
   (9 inches)
   Additional pie pastry, optional
   Whipped cream, optional

1. In a large bowl, beat the first 10 ingredients until smooth; pour into pastry shell. Cover the edge loosely with foil to prevent overbrowning.

2. Bake at 400° for 10 minutes. Reduce the heat to 350°; bake 40-45 minutes longer or until a knife inserted in the center comes out clean. Remove foil. Cool on a wire rack.

3. If decorative cutouts are desired, roll additional pastry to ⅛-in. thickness; cut out with 1-1½-in. leaf-shaped cookie cutters. With a sharp knife, score leaf veins on cutouts.

4. Place on an ungreased baking sheet. Bake at 400° for 6-8 minutes or until golden brown. Remove to a wire rack to cool. Arrange around edge of pie. Garnish with whipped cream if desired.

* Learn how to make homemade whipped cream on page 27.

HOW TO MAKE DECORATIVE PIE CRUSTS

If you want to get fancy with your pie crust, here's how! First, if you decide to make the 9-inch pie crust from scratch: Combine 1¼ cups all-purpose flour and ¼ teaspoon salt; cut in ½ cup cold butter until crumbly. Gradually add 3-5 tablespoons ice water, tossing with a fork until dough holds together when pressed. Wrap in plastic and refrigerate for 1 hour. Roll to ⅛-inch-thick circle; transfer to pie pan.

Ruffle edge: Turn the overhanging pie pastry under to form a rolled edge. Position a thumb and index finger about 1 in. apart on the outside edge of the crust, pointing in. Position the index finger of your other hand between the two fingers and gently push the pastry toward the edge. Continue around edge.

Sunflower edge: Trim the pie pastry even with the edge of a pie plate. Hold a teaspoon or tablespoon (whatever you prefer!) upside down and roll the tip of the spoon around the edge of the pastry, cutting it. Remove and toss the cut pieces. Beautiful!

REFERENCE GUIDES

Find exactly what you need to be the cook you always knew you could be. If you're unfamiliar with a food term, see the following guide. Out of an ingredient? Turn the page to discover an easy substitution. If you're looking for a specific recipe or how-to, check out the indexes.

COOKING TERMS

AL DENTE An Italian term meaning "to the tooth." Used to describe pasta that is cooked but still firm.

BASTE To moisten food with melted butter, pan drippings, marinade or other liquid to add flavor and juiciness.

BEAT To mix rapidly with a spoon, fork, wire whisk or electric mixer.

BLEND To combine ingredients until just mixed.

BOIL To heat liquids until bubbles that cannot be stirred down are formed. In the case of water, the temperature will reach 212 degrees.

BONE To remove all bones from meat, poultry or fish.

BROIL To cook food 4-6 inches from a direct, radiant heat source.

CREAM To blend ingredients to a smooth consistency by beating; frequently done with butter and sugar for baking.

CUT IN To break down and distribute cold butter, margarine or shortening into a flour mixture with a pastry blender or two knives.

DASH A measurement less than ⅛ teaspoon that is used for herbs, spices and hot pepper sauce. This is not a precise measurement.

DREDGE To coat foods with flour or other dry ingredients. Most often done with pot roasts and stew meat before browning.

FLUTE To make a "V" shape or scalloped edge on pie crust with your thumb and fingers.

FOLD To blend dissimilar ingredients by careful and gentle turning with a spatula. Used most commonly to incorporate whipped cream, beaten egg whites, fruit, candy or nuts into a thick, heavy batter.

JULIENNE To cut foods into long thin strips much like matchsticks. Used often for salads and stir-fries.

KNEAD To work dough by using a pressing and folding action to make it smooth and elastic.

MARINATE To tenderize and/or flavor foods, usually vegetables or raw meat, by placing them in a mixture of oil, vinegar, wine, lime or lemon juice, herbs and spices.

MINCE To cut into very fine pieces. Often used for garlic, hot peppers and fresh herbs.

PARBOIL To boil foods, usually vegetables, until partially cooked. Most often used when vegetables are to be finished using another cooking method or chilled for marinated salads or dips.

PINCH A measurement less than ⅛ teaspoon that is easily held between the thumb and index finger. This is not a precise measurement.

PULSE To process foods in a food processor or blender with short bursts of power.

PUREE To mash solid foods into a smooth mixture with a food processor, mill, blender or sieve.

SAUTE To fry quickly in a small amount of fat, stirring almost constantly. Most often done with onions, mushrooms and other chopped vegetables.

SCORE To cut slits partway through the outer surface of foods. Often required for ham or flank steak.

SIMMER To cook liquids, or a combination of ingredients with liquid, at just under the boiling point (180-200°). The surface of the liquid will have some movement and there may be small bubbles around the sides of the pan.

STEAM To cook foods covered on a rack or in a steamer basket over a small amount of boiling water. Most often used for vegetables.

STIR-FRY To cook meats, grains and/or vegetables with a constant stirring motion, in a small amount of oil, in a wok or skillet over high heat.

EQUIVALENT MEASURES

3 teaspoons	= 1 tablespoon	**16 tablespoons**	= 1 cup
4 tablespoons	= ¼ cup	**2 cups**	= 1 pint
5⅓ tablespoons	= ⅓ cup	**4 cups**	= 1 quart
8 tablespoons	= ½ cup	**4 quarts**	= 1 gallon

FOOD EQUIVALENTS

Macaroni	1 cup (3½ ounces) uncooked	= 2½ cups cooked
Noodles, Medium	3 cups (4 ounces) uncooked	= 4 cups cooked
Popcorn	⅓ - ½ cup unpopped	= 8 cups popped
Rice, Long Grain	1 cup uncooked	= 3 cups cooked
Rice, Quick-Cooking	1 cup uncooked	= 2 cups cooked
Spaghetti	8 ounces uncooked	= 4 cups cooked
Bread	1 slice	= ¾ cup soft crumbs, ¼ cup fine dry crumbs
Graham Crackers	7 squares	= ½ cup finely crushed
Buttery Round Crackers	12 crackers	= ½ cup finely crushed
Saltine Crackers	14 crackers	= ½ cup finely crushed
Bananas	1 medium	= ⅓ cup mashed
Lemons	1 medium	= 3 tablespoons juice, 2 teaspoons grated peel
Limes	1 medium	= 2 tablespoons juice, 1½ teaspoons grated peel
Oranges	1 medium	= ¼ -⅓ cup juice, 4 teaspoons grated peel

Cabbage	1 head = 5 cups shredded	**Green Pepper**	1 large = 1 cup chopped
Carrots	1 pound = 3 cups shredded	**Mushrooms**	½ pound = 3 cups sliced
Celery	1 rib = ½ cup chopped	**Onions**	1 medium = ½ cup chopped
Corn	1 ear fresh = ⅔ cup kernels	**Potatoes**	3 medium = 2 cups cubed
Almonds	1 pound = 3 cups chopped	**Pecan Halves**	1 pound = 4½ cups chopped
Ground Nuts	3¾ ounces = 1 cup	**Walnuts**	1 pound = 3¾ cups chopped

EASY SUBSTITUTIONS

WHEN YOU NEED...		USE...
Baking Powder	1 teaspoon	½ teaspoon cream of tartar + ¼ teaspoon baking soda
Buttermilk	1 cup	1 tablespoon lemon juice or vinegar + enough milk to measure 1 cup (let stand 5 minutes before using)
Cornstarch	1 tablespoon	2 tablespoons all-purpose flour
Honey	1 cup	1¼ cups sugar + ¼ cup water
Half-and-Half Cream	1 cup	1 tablespoon melted butter + enough whole milk to measure 1 cup
Onion	1 small, chopped (⅓ cup)	1 teaspoon onion powder or 1 tablespoon dried minced onion
Tomato Juice	1 cup	½ cup tomato sauce + ½ cup water
Tomato Sauce	2 cups	¾ cup tomato paste + 1 cup water
Unsweetened Chocolate	1 square (1 ounce)	3 tablespoons baking cocoa + 1 tablespoon shortening or oil
Whole Milk	1 cup	½ cup evaporated milk + ½ cup water

HOW-TO'S & HINTS INDEX

RECIPE INDEX